LIFE ONE-0-ONE
Find your Purpose
www.lifeone0one.com
vince@lifeone0one.com

LIFE ONE-0-ONE

Find Your Purpose

BUILDING BLOCKS

FOR A HEALTHY, HAPPY AND FULFILLING LIFE

Vince DaCosta

Copyright © 2009 by Vince DaCosta

All rights reserved. No part of this book shall be reproduced or transmitted in any form or by any means, electronic, mechanical, magnetic, photographic including photocopying, recording or by any information storage and retrieval system, without prior written permission of the publisher. No patent liability is assumed with respect to the use of the information contained herein. Although every precaution has been taken in the preparation of this book, the publisher and author assume no responsibility for errors or omissions. Neither is any liability assumed for damages resulting from the use of the information contained herein.

ISBN 0-7414-5480-7

Published by:

1094 New DeHaven Street, Suite 100
West Conshohocken, PA 19428-2713
Info@buybooksontheweb.com
www.buybooksontheweb.com
Toll-free (877) BUY BOOK
Local Phone (610) 941-9999
Fax (610) 941-9959

Printed in the United States of America

Published August 2009

To:
my four beautiful grandchildren...
Justin, Alicia, Adrianna and Matthew
to help you find your life's Purpose.

There are only two ways to live your life.
One is as though nothing is a miracle.
The other is as though everything is a miracle

Albert Einstein

They said . . . .

I have known Vince DaCosta for over 20 years. To describe him I would have to use words like innovator, grounded, happy, committed, funny, passionate and directed. In his speeches, seminars and books he delivers reliable, real-world techniques for anyone to enjoy more of life. This book is no different. A wonderful read! In "LIFE ONE-0-ONE: Find Your Purpose", you will find a practical guidebook to discover the all important questions, "Why am I here and how can I live my life with purpose."

- Gerry Robert
Best-Selling Author of The Millionaire Mindset

Vince DaCosta is one of the outstanding members of our Continuing Education Team. We presented him with the prestigious Humber College "Award of Excellence for Outstanding Academic Contribution." Vince's students returned time and time again to experience the inspiration and motivation of his life skills training workshops. His new book, "LIFE ONE-0-ONE: Find your Purpose" contains the essence of Vince's teachings. Read it to lift your life to a higher level of peace, happiness and joy.

- Jane Russ / Manager
Humber Institute of Technology & Advanced Learning

Vince DaCosta has conducted hundreds of training workshops and seminars with Diamond Institute. Vince has helped many of our students start a new life with his comprehensive and uplifting life courses. His new book "LIFE ONE-0-ONE: Find your Purpose" is another step in the direction of Vince's mission to help People Achieve. This is a must read for a fulfilling and successful life.

- Joe Gagliardi / President,
Diamond Institute of Business and Computer Technology.

Acknowledgments

Writing this book was a joyful experience of discovery. There were epiphanies, surprises and moments of awe, as I looked back at experiences and discoveries I made along the road of my life. However, my book could not have been completed without the help and support of many people.

First on my list is my dear wife Hyacinth. "Thank you for the many days you waited patiently as I sat at my desk researching, reminiscing and recalling experiences from the past." She gave support and encouragement, and I needed it. With her penchant for detail she quickly found the errors and omissions I kept overlooking.

Thanks to Patricia Codner, my editor, niece and dear friend, for the countless hours spent reading and re-reading all the chapters. She identified so many instances where change was necessary. Thanks also for the encouragement and inspiration when my energy and confidence flagged.

Thanks to my associate Marcello Scarsella with his sharp mind and ready humour, but most of all for his critical and crucial advice. My list also includes the students and workshop participants who questioned and challenged my ideas through the years. Thanks to those of you who kept on asking when I would start my second book. Well, here it is.

Thanks to my precious daughters Rosalie and Sheila and their faithful husbands Marcello and Vincenzo, who make me proud to be a father. I love them, even though I don't say so as much as I should. Finally, thanks to those of like faith who believe as I do that there is an endless day ahead, and this is just the beginning.

Thank you all, for your helpful advice, inspiration and love.

LIFE ONE-0-ONE:

Find Your Purpose

Contents

Introduction   P. 1

Chapter 1
9 Building Blocks to a Winning Attitude   P. 5

Chapter 2
9 Building Blocks to Beliefs for Success and Happiness   P. 26

Chapter 3
6 Building Blocks to Meaning and Purpose   P. 45

Chapter 4
7 Building Blocks to Gratitude that Heals   P. 61

Chapter 5
6 Building Blocks to Higher Consciousness   P. 76

Chapter 6
7 Building Blocks to Love, Joy and Peace   P. 88

Chapter 7
Getting safely to The Beginning   P. 104

Introduction

"Why didn't they tell me this in school?"

This is the question I consistently hear from participants in workshops and seminars I conduct. They are surprised that some of the basic strategies for living a happy, successful and fulfilling life are never mentioned during school days. They enter the work world, thinking they are well equipped for the journey of life, only to find that important things are still missing.

The road to a safe and happy life is not complex or mysterious. It does not require a PhD. or a fortune in the bank. *"Life One-0-One: Find your Purpose"* is about people who discovered that happiness and satisfaction does not depend on fame and fortune. What they found was, that positive attitudes and character attract respect and admiration in both personal and professional life. What they also discovered was a certain significance and meaning to their lives. They found their life's purpose, and experienced the peace of mind and rest they had longed for. They finally found their place in the grand scheme of things.

One of the major building blocks on the road to happiness is Attitude. Most educators agree that Attitude represents 85% of a person's success. Without the communication skills to relate and influence others, your ability to win cooperation and support is limited.

Another major building block is Belief. Our beliefs must support our vision of success. We must get rid of beliefs that burden us with fear and doubt.

How to identify and delete negative beliefs, and program your subconscious for success-beliefs is an important building block towards happiness and peace of mind.

"The purpose of life . . . . is a life of purpose!" Without a meaning and purpose to life, the whole exercise becomes pointless. Those without a purpose become bored, frustrated, discouraged and distressed. In chapter 3 we look at your personal purpose, and then beyond to the ultimate purpose of the Universe.

This finely engineered, exquisitely planned Universe has been planned to the degree that one tiny fraction of difference in its structure would cause it to fall apart. Listen to one of the world's most famous biologists, Dr. Robert Lanza: "Modern science cannot explain why the laws of physics are exactly balanced for animal life to exist. For example, if the Big Bang had been one-part-in-a-billion more powerful, it would have rushed out too fast for the galaxies to form and for life to begin. If the strong nuclear force were decreased by two percent, atomic nuclei wouldn't hold together. Hydrogen would be the only atom in the Universe. If the gravitational force were decreased, stars (including the sun) would not ignite. These are just three of more than 200 physical parameters within the solar system and Universe so exact that they cannot be random."

At this very moment the goal of the scientific community is trying to answer the question, "Is there a Purpose?" They have dug deep, looking for what is called The Theory of Everything. Their search has led them deep inside the atom that was thought to be the genesis of all matter. Surprise! Surprise!!

Introduction

Turns out the atom is a world unto itself. Inside the atom are electrons, protons and neutrons. These subatomic parts are so small that in proportion the atom is as large as a football field, and the atom is something you cannot see with your naked eye.

They dug deeper and found that there is something smaller than these subatomic parts. They are called quarks. A quark is so small that our minds cannot conceive its size. It is beyond infinitesimal.

Over in Geneva, Switzerland scientists are about to test a $5 Billion Hadron Collider atom smasher and hope to find something smaller than a quark. There seems to be no limit to how small subatomic parts are. Just as it seems there is no limit to how large the Universe is.

I believe the purpose of the Universe is quite simple. It doesn't need an Einstein or a Darwin to tell us. If we pause and become quiet in our minds and our hearts, the answer comes. The Universe is specially designed and balanced for human beings to exist. It is the perfect school for us humans to make choices that can transform our lives to a higher consciousness. I believe that we all hear the call to reach for that higher consciousness but most of us ignore it. We prefer to wander on in the passions and pressures of our lower nature. We prefer to live by instinct. Jesus, the Great Teacher said, "Men loved darkness rather than light."

Vince DaCosta

Chapter 1

BUILD A WINNING ATTITUDE

9 Building Blocks

On March 22, 1982 I had an epiphany.
    I didn't know it at the time. It was only as the days and weeks went by, that I began to realize that something profound had taken place in my life. There was nothing startling about the epiphany. Actually, it was just a few words spoken by a student in a training workshop I was conducting. The student probably had no idea that she had spoken words that would dramatically affect my outlook and behaviour; words that would set me on a path away from frustration, disappointment and failure, and start me on a road leading to peace of mind, success and happiness.
    On that memorable day we were discussing Attitude in the training workshop. There were about fifteen to twenty participants. We discussed the suggestion of experts that Attitude is more important than Skills and Knowledge. We talked about the famous words of Charles Swindoll in his poem on Attitude: *"Attitude, to me is more important than facts. It is more important than the past, than education, than money, than circumstances, than failures, than successes, than what other people think or say or do. It is more important than appearance, giftedness or skill. It will make or break a company . . . a church . . . a home."*

We discussed the teachings of some of the great educators of our day. Teachers such as Stephen Covey, Zig Ziglar, Brian Tracy, Norman Vince Peale and others who maintain that 85% of our success is the result of our Attitude.

> **Attitude is a Habit of Thought**

We finally came to the crucial question, "What is Attitude? How can we define it?" A number of students suggested, "It's how we act." Some thought it was a gift from our parents. Others thought it was the result of the environment in which we were born. After a long pause, one student said, "Attitude is a Habit of Thought". I asked her to repeat that. I had never heard it put like that before. I liked the sound of it: I wrote it on the board: **"Attitude is a habit of thought."** I did not immediately grasp the depth and wisdom of the statement. "A habit of thought!" Little did I know at that time and in that day, that those words would change my life. Little did I know that a new day had dawned and a whole new paradigm had started to replace the old paradigm of fear, failure and loss. What a day that was on March 22, 1982!!

➤ Another Epiphany!
What a day that was for Earl Nightingale on June 9, 1950.

Earl Nightingale was one of the great educators of the twentieth century. He was born during the Great Depression and saw enormous poverty and suffering. All around him there was hunger, pain and misery. He became obsessed with finding the answer to wealth, success, and peace of mind. Surely there was an answer to the suffering and pain he saw everywhere. He began a great Search! He frequented the libraries and educational centres of that day. He listened to the voices of the wise and intelligent. He studied the literature and learning that was available. Slowly but surely he began to find an underlying message and theme in the religious, philosophical and psychological literature he was studying. In the verses of the Bible, in the sayings of Buddha, in the writings of Lao Tse, the message was clear and distinct. He marvelled that it took so long for him to find it. Maybe there was a reason why his eyes had been blinded. But now he could see clearly. Oh so clearly!

> We become what we Think About

The answer was and is: **"we become what we think about"** That was his Epiphany! He called it The Strangest Secret. ***"We become what we think about"***. Strange because it wasn't a secret at all, but rather a message he had read and heard over and over again. He recalled Ralph Waldo Emerson saying, "A man is what he thinks about all day long." He remembered Dr. Norman Vincent Peale in his Sunday sermons emphasizing ". . . . . if you think in negative terms you will get negative results. If you think in positive terms you will achieve positive results . . . " He thought of the words in the Bible, "As he thinketh in his heart, so is he." No! It really was not a secret.

Earl Nightingale knew that multitudes of people had never really understood the message clearly. He put the words on tape and sold millions of copies. Eventually The Strangest Secret became so famous and demand increased so dramatically that the recording received a Gold Record. The only talk recording ever to receive a Gold Record.

Learn how to Think

As a young boy I did not give too much significance to thoughts or thinking. Thinking happened. That was the way it was. We had thoughts, and luckily no one could see them. My thoughts were a confused jumble of school, parents, girls, food and fun. I spent a lot of time thinking about the past. I was proud of my scholastic achievements, and I played over and over in my mind soccer activities, athletic successes and other achievements. I often pictured the countries I wanted to visit one day: Egypt, China, and Japan. That was fun for me, picturing the different scenarios and wondering if I would ever see them. Thinking was fun.

In my first book, Influence, Persuade and **Win**, I told a story about my old school Principal. One day in a boring class of Latin verbs and phrases, he said, "You may never need Latin verbs and phrases in the future, but we are doing it now ***to teach you how to think***". This seemed strange to me at that time. I didn't think I needed to learn how to think. I thought I did it very well. Drifting off mentally to scenes of school activities was my perception of thinking. Dreaming of one day visiting the Pyramids of Egypt and the Great Wall of China was also thinking. Reminiscing about times with my father fishing by the seashore on pleasant summer days was thinking. What was there to learn about that? One didn't learn how to think. One just thought.

The great mass of people never learn how to think. Most of us live our lives with instinct like the wild animals and the birds. We think of danger. We think of food and shelter. We think of the things that harm and hurt. But beyond that, few of us become aware of the capacity of thought to bring purpose and meaning into our lives. Few of us learn to control our thoughts and marshal our abilities to bring success and happiness. Instead, we unconsciously develop habits of thinking which lead us nowhere and we end up angry and frustrated. In short, we allow our minds to control us, and quite often lead us to despair, worry and failure.

Your Greatest Gift

The greatest gift we have as human beings is not our health! That does not mean that health is unimportant. In the same way relationships are important, but not our greatest gift. Also faith, hope and peace of mind, all treasures we yearn for, but still not our greatest gift.

Our greatest gift is our ability to choose our thoughts. Each of us has been given the power to reject the thoughts we choose to reject, and to entertain the thoughts we choose to entertain. Without this gift to choose, we would be like the wild animals and birds. Our behaviour and life would be pre-programmed from cradle to grave. We would have no say in how we live. Every moment of everyday would be programmed and predictable. We would be locked in a fixed and predetermined behaviour, similar to the inborn tendencies of the animals. We would be creatures of instinct.

Choice of thought allows us to live our lives creatively; to envision a path and create a new life for ourselves. Some choose a path that leads to destruction, a life of selfishness, anger and revenge. Some choose to fly with eagles and reach the limits of human endeavour. They learn to love and to forgive. They choose to spend their lives for the benefit of mankind. They become a Nelson Mandela, a Mahatma Gandhi, or a Mother Teresa. Others choose the low road, and destroy themselves while destroying others. They become a Hitler.

> The Law of Attraction

You and I are like the captain of a great ocean liner. In the same way he chooses the course that will take his ship to a safe harbour, is the same way we can choose the thoughts that steer us towards peace of mind, hope and health. Conversely, we can carelessly choose the thoughts that steer us towards the rocks of frustration and failure.

A young man stands on the threshold of life. His father and mother have instilled in him by example and by persuasion, the value of respect for others. He has seen respect lived out before him in his formative years and he has developed a habit of thought about respect. As he leaves home to start his own life, it's his choice to continue to think and express that behaviour of respect. He has had a good start! Through parental help he was able to develop a way of thinking that formed a good attitude. As he moves among his peers and coworkers his attitude, his respect for himself and others is admired by everyone. What is on the inside begins to show on the outside. His peers respond positively to him, mirroring his positive behaviour. This is the Law of Attraction in action. There is nothing mystical or magical about it, nothing complicated or difficult. His positive attitude has prompted a positive response from others.

It all starts with you. Can you control your thoughts until they become "a habit of thought?" Can you control your thoughts until they become a pattern of behaviour? Successful people learn to control their thoughts and develop positive attitudes that attract positive people and positive situations.

The Greatest Discovery

William James is often referred to as the father of American Psychology. One of his most famous quotes is: **"The greatest discovery of my**

generation is that a human being can alter his life by altering his attitude of mind."

"The greatest discovery of my generation!" That's quite a statement to make. Was he saying that changing our thought patterns could change our lives? That developing a positive "habit of thought" could help us start a new and better chapter in our tomorrows? Is there evidence for this? You be the judge.

A few years ago a friend of mine, Gerry Robert, wrote a book in which he shared his personal experience. I'll let Gerry tell you as he wrote it in his book, *"Conquering life's obstacles":*

➢ Gerry's Story

"I grew up in a home with a father who suffered from alcoholism. We lived in "the project", a fancy name for low-rental development, rampant with crime, drugs and violence. At ten years of age, adults encouraged me to steal. I didn't let them down. I enjoyed the attention.

In the years that followed things grew worse, considerably worse. At thirteen, a friend showed me some white pills he had bought with money from a stolen purse. They made me forget the pain. During the "trip" I didn't think about what was happening. I could escape for a while. I fell in love with "intoxication". I was in that condition as frequently and as intensely as I could be, even at that young age. I was drinking in bars at fifteen and was kicked out of school that year too and I started working full-time just before my sixteenth birthday.

I had my first run-in with the police that year. I was arrested and convicted for grand theft auto. By the time I was eighteen, I had committed many crimes including shoplifting, kidnapping, drug trafficking, abduction and armed robbery.

In February 1977 I was arrested for armed robbery. **On September 6, 1977 however, my life was turned around forever.** It is a day I will never forget! On that day, I left the life of crime and deceit. I got off the road of failure and got on the road of success. I left negative thinking behind and chose positive thinking instead. On that very special day I began to change from a life of destruction, despair and poverty to enjoy a life of value, happiness and prosperity."

Powerful words! Words of hope, faith and victory. As Gerry Robert says, if he can do it, so can any of us on this planet. The sequel to Gerry's remarkable story is that today he is in demand all over the World, telling his story of how he altered his attitude and altered his life.

When I tell Gerry's story to audiences, there nearly always is someone who comes to me after the presentation to tell me privately that they were in much the same condition and experience as Gerry. However, through discipline and desire they were able to alter their attitude and alter their lives.

> The Prison of Negativity

But sadly, there are many, too many, who never discover the tremendous power of their "greatest gift." I worked with a beautiful, capable and promising young woman for many years. Unfortunately, underneath all that beauty lurked a destructive threat. She had a "habit of thought" that she was worthless. That she would not and could not be successful. That she would not and could not ever be loved. That she was not worthy of anyone's admiration and respect. Despite all the advice of others that she was just like any other worthy human being, and could achieve whatever she wanted, she retreated more and more into herself. Eventually, she gave up and died, but we couldn't bury her, because she was still breathing. All her faith, joy and hope had died. Life was now a tedious, pointless and painful wait for the final breath. We tried to reach her, but she had closed the doors of communication and lived in her own world of negativity and failure. Finally she stopped breathing and we buried her.

Have you put yourself into the prison of negativity and failure? Have you lost all hope, and shut yourself away in the prison of your mind? William James maintains, along with all the educators and Gerry Robert, that you can alter your life by altering your attitudes of thought. That was his epiphany!

Most people are not aware of what makes their lives unhappy and without meaning. Most people are not aware of what makes them feel lost. They keep on doing the same things, thinking the same thoughts and hoping for change in their experience. They remain unaware that they are attracting their condition to themselves. They have not accepted the universal truth "If you keep on doing what you are doing, you will keep on getting what you are getting." They are like the people in the Blacksmith Story. I like to tell the Blacksmith Story to audiences. My hope is that it will break through closed minds and mind sets and shine the light of awareness on the cause of continuing failure.

> ➤ The Blacksmith Story

Once upon a time long ago, when men rode to work on horses, and women stayed at home, there lived a very wise man. He lived a simple life, working long hard hours at his trade, mending the chariot wheels and fixing the shoes the horses wore. The sign on his little shop said:

<u>BLACKSMITH</u>

One day a man rode up on his horse and said, "Blacksmith, fix my horse's shoe, I think it's broken." "Yes Sir", said the blacksmith, "I'll have it done quickly." The man seemed impatient and uncomfortable, and after some time he approached the blacksmith with a question. "Blacksmith" he said, "I intend to spend a few days in your village on business. Tell me, what kind of people live in your village?" The blacksmith thought for a moment, and then answered with another question. "What kind of people live in the town where you came from?" "Oh," said the man, "they were very difficult people. I found them quite rude and disrespectful. Some were even cynical and critical of my product. One man insulted me."

The blacksmith gave an understanding sigh as he said; "I have bad news for you, Sir. I think you will find the people in our village, just like the people you met in the town where you came from. They probably will be just as cynical and critical, just as rude and disrespectful as those you met in the town you came from." The man seemed angry and muttered under his breath, "Seems everywhere I go people are rude and critical. I just don't understand."

The blacksmith smiled knowingly, as he completed the job and bid the man goodbye.

It was late in the afternoon when a lady rode up in her horse and buggy. She was distraught. "I hope you can help me Mr. Blacksmith. All along the road my buggy wheel has been wobbling, and I am worried that it might fall off." "Not to worry," said the blacksmith, "we'll soon have you on your way again," and he smiled a comforting smile. The lady seemed relieved, and thanked him for his interest. After a while she explained to him that she would be in the village for a few days on business and she was just wondering, "What kind of people live in your town?" Again the blacksmith answered her question with his question: "What kind of people live in the town where you came from?" "I'm glad you asked that question," she said. "I'll not forget those people, they were so kind, they were so respectful, and they were so sensitive and considerate. I must go back there again." "I have good news for you" said the blacksmith. "In my village you will find the people just as kind, just as considerate, just as respectful as the people in the town where you came from", and he wished her a good day as he completed the job and bid her goodbye.

➢ Getting the best from People

That night the blacksmith told his wife about his experience. He told her about the man who had a bad experience, and the woman who had a good experience. He told her it was a picture of people and their world. He told her that some people as they walk life's road, consistently get the best that people have to offer. They get kindness, respect, appreciation and love. Others as they travel the same road get the worst that people have to offer.

They get criticism, cynicism, disrespect and rejection. "Why is that?" asked the blacksmith's wife. Said the blacksmith, "because some learn the power of a positive Attitude and some never become aware of the negative Attitude they have."

Think of the kind of people that live in the town you came from, the school that you attend, the job that you have and the church that you go to. What kind of people are they? Kind, trusting and respectful? Or could they be critical, unappreciative and unkind? Is there a chance they might be reflecting the attitude that you are showing them? Is it possible that you are attracting the behaviour that they are showing you?

I am always quick to point out to people when they speak of having a great manager, supervisor or friend, that they have a lot to do with that relationship. Maybe quite unconsciously they are communicating a positive, appreciative attitude, and their manager, supervisor and friend is merely reflecting it back to them. The Law of Attraction at work again!

Proactive People

My parents had a profound effect on my life. They protected me from negative influences and warned me about inappropriate friendships. "Birds of a feather, flock together", they kept telling me over and over again. They knew that if I got in with the wrong crowd, it wouldn't be long before I was in the wrong places. Mom and Dad were proactive people They looked ahead and saw the danger signs and had a plan to help me manage them.

To alter attitudes we need to associate with positive, proactive people, knowing that their interaction will have a profound effect on our thinking. That's what I did when I joined Toastmasters International. As I met with this positive, proactive and ambitious group of people, I could tell that with exposure to them I would take on some of their attitudes and spirit. Its been thirty years, and I know I should have made more progress, but I attribute much of my success to the members of that great organization.

➤ Fail to Plan and You Plan to Fail

One of the most respected universities in North America conducted a survey to find out more about proactive people. In 1953 Harvard University interviewed the graduating students that year, and asked each person to describe their plans for the future. Did they have a plan? Was the plan specific and realistic? Had they written it down or was it just a dream? Were they casual or passionate about the plan?

Only 3 percent of those graduating students had a specific, realistic written plan. The rest had a variety of excuses for plans. Some had no plans at all. Amazing! They had spent four or five gruelling years, sleepless nights and lonely days preparing for their future and at the end of it all they really didn't know where they were going.

The University filed away the results of the survey. Twenty years later in 1973 they went back and interviewed each student to find out how well they were doing in the real world. They made an amazing discovery. The 3 percent who had learned the importance of being proactive, had achieved more in financial and spiritual terms than the other 97 percent combined. Dramatic evidence of the common phrase, "Fail to plan, and you plan to Fail". The 3 percent students had formed a habit of thinking and visualizing the future and preparing for it. They had developed positive proactive attitudes.

So, what about the 97 percent students? Were they all failures? Probably not, but they were much more open to reactive tendencies. Reactive people tend to blame and complain. They see the "glass as half empty", meaning they see the potential for failure first. They tend to wait on things to happen in contrast to proactive people who make things happen. The 3 percent students see the "glass as half full". When we see the potential for success first as we face challenges, we give it a determined try. We keep trying because we know there is potential for success. Reactive people stop trying because they see themselves failing. So we are back again to our "habit of thought"

Self-Development Books

If you have a University degree, I applaud you. I applaud the discipline, determination and courage it took to achieve your degree. It will stand you in good stead and will open doors of opportunity in the future.

If you don't have a University degree, do not despair. All the information that you need to achieve post University status is available and it's absolutely free. The public libraries in the cities of North America and other countries of the World are overflowing with all the knowledge you will ever need, and as I said it's free.

It always amazes me how casual some people are with the opportunities for learning at their disposal. Libraries contain millions of books that tell stories of success, happiness and achievement. Some of the great educators and teachers have willingly shared their knowledge and experiences. Some had to struggle with much the same problems and challenges we encounter, and the story of how they overcame is in a book somewhere.

Prominent among self-development books is Dale Carnegie's, *"How to win Friends and Influence People"*. This is a must read for young and old, written in simple language, describing and extolling the art of getting along with people. Something a little more academic would be Steven Covey's *"7 Habits of highly Effective People"*, another manual of wisdom and knowledge on building better relationships. The list is endless and the knowledge infinite. All it requires is the commitment to improvement.

Today's world demands that we join the movement towards Continuing Education. This means constant upgrading and reinforcing our knowledge, and there is a whole industry devoted to meeting that need. So join the march to your nearest library and begin to further your knowledge in your chosen field.

I know that of which I speak. My school years were spent more on the soccer field than in the classroom. My perception of success was not getting good grades, but rather running the 100 meter race in record time The result was that when I left I had a lot of catching up to do, and that's when I found out about libraries. I became a veritable bookworm. Today books are my friend and I love to saunter through bookstores and libraries and savour the latest updates in knowledge.

Positive Self-Talk

Dr. Wilder Penfield was one of Canada's most prestigious and famous neurosurgeons. In 1928 he joined the faculty of McGill University in Montreal where he became known worldwide for his research and experiments on the human brain.

One of Dr. Penfield's greatest achievements was a procedure known as the "Montreal Procedure". During this operation Dr. Penfield worked on the patient's brain while the patient was conscious. You could say it was open brain surgery with a conscious patient. Dr. Penfield, using electrical probes stimulated parts of the patient's brain and the patient responded audibly with a memory or thought of a past event. Moving the probe to different parts of the brain elicited different memories and thoughts. Dr. Penfield was literally looking at the patient's thoughts in the past.

If Dr. Penfield were with us today I would ask him to use the Montreal Procedure on two people who I know very well. They are a sister and brother,

Juanita and Manuel. They had the same Father and Mother, same home environment, went to the same school, but chose different "habits of thought".

> I am a Beautiful Person

Here is the scenario that would unfold as Dr. Penfield stimulates a certain part of Juanita's brain: He would hear her repeating these words, "I am very plain. I feel ugly" Moving his probe to another area of her brain he would hear, "nobody loves me. I feel lonely." A few more movements of his probe and he would hear these thoughts and memories: "I will never succeed." "I wish I was someone else." "I am sorry I was ever born."

Sadly this has all come to pass in Juanita's life. She became what she consistently thought about. Today she is a lonely recluse, hiding away from others. In effect, she is hiding away from life.

But what of Manuel? Dr Penfield is probing Manuel's brain. He smiles as he stimulates a certain area and hears Manuel say, "I am a beautiful person". He quickly touches another area and is excited to hear Manuel say, "I am thankful for health and happiness." He moves on to hear more. "Today is a beautiful day." "There are miracles all around me." "I am a miracle."

Manuel grew up to be that confident and successful person he kept talking to himself about. He developed confidence and courage. When disappointments and problems came, he kept saying, "I'll keep trying and tomorrow will be better." Today he is a pleasure to be with.

What would Dr. Penfield hear you saying if he had a chance to stimulate your brain and bring out the thoughts and memories that you are carrying in your mind? What would a "Montreal Procedure" reveal? What does your Self-Talk sound like?

Here are a few powerful strategies for improving your Self Talk and building a more positive attitude.

Control your thoughts
Remember, you are in control. That is your greatest gift. When we allow our minds and thoughts to control us, we are on the road to disaster. That disaster includes Fear, Worry and Mental breakdown. Too many in our World today are already there.

Use an "A" card
Write a positive Affirmation on a 3 X 5 card and keep it with you always. Read it often. "I am a beautiful person" may be a good affirmation to start with.
Here are a few more:
- I always do my best
- My services are valuable
- I am a vibrant person
- I think big and choose to help others

Analyse your day
Before you go to bed each night, review the day and analyse how you did. Were there more positive thoughts than negatives? Were there any positive thoughts at all?

Watch the Media
Experts say that bad news sells 5 times faster than good news, so there is no mystery why most of our news is negative. Close the door of your mind and shut out the confusion and distress. We may need to

be aware of the events that are taking place, but we certainly do not need to allow them to drown us with fear and worry.

➢ A New World

In 1492 Christopher Columbus sailed away from the shores of Spain, entering the unknown waters of the Atlantic Ocean. Never before had anyone dared to explore those waters. Columbus thought that if he sailed far enough and long enough he would come back to Spain, since he knew the world was round. Instead, he landed on shores where no European had ever been before. He discovered a New World. America!

In 1982 when I heard the words "Attitude is a habit of thought", I hardly realized then that I too was discovering a whole New World. I began to appreciate more, the secret that all successful people know: "You become what you think about". The awareness of these fundamental concepts surprised me with their simplicity and logic. I recognized that it was time to seek out positive people to help me change my "habits of thought" that had become so much a part of me. Only those who have been there can understand the struggle to break the old habits of thought and nurture a new more mature and positive attitude. As I worked with others and myself, with positive self-talk and affirmations, I began to realize that I was leaving my old world behind for a new one. Confidence flourished, courage was strengthened and a future that I had only dreamt of began to take form. I learned to forgive and to forget. I refused to let shame and blame destroy me. I lifted myself up on the wings of hope and faith, and learned to find contentment and peace. At last I was at rest, in a wonderful New World.

9 Building Blocks for a Winning Attitude

- Attitude is a habit of thought
- We become what we think about
- Learn how to think
- Your Greatest Gift
- The Greatest Discovery
- Awareness
- Proactive People
- Self-Development books
- Positive Self Talk

Chapter 2

BELIEFS TO SUCCEED

9 Building Blocks

I was born with a curious mind!

I have always had a seemingly insatiable hunger for the answer to the mystery of life. This yearning for truth has prompted me to read every book, listen to every person, follow through on every advertisement that promised the answer. At times I have found myself with people who were so sure they knew, but were no further ahead than I was.

Through all these experiences I began to notice a common thread. There always seemed to be one stubborn and undeniable factor, which kept repeating time and time again. The authors and teachers all believed they were right. They all maintained that they were in possession of absolute truth. They all believed they had found the answer.

➢ The Way we Think

Gradually I began to realize that the answer could not be in the stories that I was hearing. There were too many contradictions and inconsistencies. There were far too many "Truths". Everyone could not be right. Maybe, the answer was not in the stories. Maybe the answer to this confusion was somewhere else. Maybe the answer was in the way we think.

I believe the answer to the many "truths" held so passionately by so many cultures, religions and philosophies is in the mystery and magic of Belief.

The stories were different, but the Belief was the same. Every book, every philosophy, every doctrine represented a condition of mind that was similar. There was no doubt, no uncertainty no questions. My way is right and everyone else is wrong. I saw it in conversations with friends. I saw it in discussions on Politics, Religion and History. Always there were those who were right, and not prepared to consider any other perspective. They believed they were right, and that was it. End of story!

The Subconscious Mind

The answer to the Belief Syndrome is in the Subconscious Mind. Our mind has two parts. The conscious mind and the subconscious mind. We are constantly aware of our conscious mind. We make decisions, we analyze situations, and we jump to conclusions with our conscious mind. It is very easy to feel that our conscious mind is all that there is, but scientists say the conscious mind is only about 10% of our thinking capacity.

So where is the other 90% ? Locked away in your subconscious mind. Everything you have ever known or experienced is in your subconscious mind. Every thought, every word, every song, every harsh and angry word expressed, every loving act performed. Your subconscious is a vast storehouse of all your past experience, and has overwhelming influence on all your actions and reactions. Most of us are not aware of the subconscious or its tremendous power to bring success and happiness into our lives.

When we understand how the subconscious mind works, it can open unlimited opportunity to us. The impossible becomes possible. The subconscious mind takes any problem or challenge you have and strives to find the answer or solution. The stories are legion of dramatic discoveries that flashed into the mind of inventors and artists as they grappled with their challenges. Some speak of it as flashes of insight, which is another way of saying the subconscious is at work. Bill Gates founded Microsoft through flashes of intuition, and Napoleon the great French general, won his battles with the help of the power of his subconscious. If your goal is to have a nice home, or win new friends or get a better job, the subconscious mind will make you aware of the actions and habits you need to develop in order to reach your goal. More importantly, it will supply the courage and passion to get there.

The Gate Keeper

The conscious mind is the "gate keeper" of our mind. It analyzes and screens our thoughts, rejecting what appears to be untrue, unrealistic or impossible. It is our instrument of choice. It gives us control, and as we discussed in Chapter 1, it is our greatest gift. However it sometimes happens that an untrue, unrealistic or undesirable thought gains entrance to our conscious mind. Instead of rejecting this thought

we entertain it and it ends up in our subconscious mind. The subconscious mind welcomes this thought, but accepts it as absolutely true. The subconscious mind does not analyze, examine or reject anything. That is not its purpose. It takes this thought and begins to make it a reality in your experience. That's its job! It will translate the thoughts, desires, ambitions and plans into tangible physical results. That untrue, unrealistic, undesirable thought we allowed in our subconscious will eventually become our "truth"
Your subconscious mind is your mechanism for translating true or untrue, bad or good, kind or unkind thoughts into reality in your life.

It stands to reason then that we would want only positive, productive and life enhancing thoughts to reach our subconscious mind. That's what the next session is all about. Conditioning our subconscious mind with our dreams, hopes and plans and watch them become a reality in our lives.

➢ We are all hypnotized

Maxwell Maltz suggests that we are all hypnotized!
Dr. Maxwell Maltz was a plastic surgeon before he became a Best-Selling author. While practicing plastic surgery he noticed the dramatic changes in personality and attitude that took place in his patients as he corrected defects. Disfigured facial features sustained in some unfortunate accident were replaced with original features, and the anticipated improvements in self-esteem and confidence were restored.

But there were instances when this did not happen. Instances when a disfigured face was replaced with its original beauty and form, but the expected improvement in personality did not occur. These patients continued to act with low self-esteem, disappointment and despair. Dr. Maltz began to investigate these exceptions in his practice and was shocked to find that these patients could not "see" the changes. He showed them before and after comparison pictures, pointing to the obvious differences and the improvements. His patients responded with the statement: "The pictures may look different, but I don't feel any different." All his skill and expertise could not change the internal picture they had continued to hold in their subconscious mind. In effect, despite the obvious difference in the photographs, they still "knew" they were ugly, and they continued to act on their "truth".

The Self-Image

This changed the direction of Dr. Maltz's practice. He determined that instead of a life devoted to healing people's external faults and blemishes, he would spend the rest of his life healing people's internal blemishes. He called what he had found, the **self-image**. This is the internal picture that we hold of ourselves in our subconscious mind. He dealt with it in his famous best selling book *"Psycho-Cybernetics"*. People were hungry for what he wrote and bought over 30 million copies.

In his book, Dr. Maltz suggests that what a hypnotist does is to simply influence the belief you have. An example might be an athlete lifting a weight of 200 lbs but unable to lift 225 lbs. After hypnotizing the athlete, the hypnotist bypasses the conscious mind and goes directly to the subconscious mind, implanting the belief that the athlete can lift 250 lbs. The athlete easily lifts the 250 lb. weight. Maxwell Maltz suggests that the athlete was unable to lift 225 lbs. because he "knew" (believed) he could not. The hypnotist changed his belief and allowed him to express his true strength.

My experience in Toastmasters with public speaking is a dramatic example of being hypnotized into "knowing" I could not speak in public. The fear and apprehension I felt only helped to confirm what I already "knew". This was something that was very real to me. With time I was able to change that belief and become quite comfortable speaking to large and small audiences. Over and over again people come into the organization with the belief that they cannot speak as well as other members. With time and effort their belief changes, and they become just as proficient as other members.

The Alpha State

We can hypnotize ourselves. Actually we do it all the time. Have you ever become lost while reading a good book, or become enthralled as you watch a beautiful sunset? At moments like that, time seems to stand still. Actually, our brain wave activity slows and we enter a state which psychologists call the Alpha state. This is a state during which the electrical vibrations in our brain slow to a point where our brain and body becomes quite relaxed. During the Alpha State electrical pulses slow from approximately 30 cycles per second to approximately 10 cycles per second. This results in a daydreaming or reverie condition, during which you are highly suggestible. This is the state a hypnotist takes you to. There are thousands of websites on the Internet offering to do this for you. They usually are selling a CD with music or voice which relaxes you as it makes suggestions while you are in the Alpha state.

You can do this for yourself. Every night as you drift off to sleep, you experience a few moments just before losing consciousness when there is still some awareness of your surroundings. You are not fully awake, but neither are you fully asleep. Actually, you are in the Alpha state. You experience the same condition as you awake in the morning. During the Alpha state your subconscious mind is more open to suggestion. This is the state of mind a hypnotist takes you to. You can now become the hypnotist and consciously program your mind with your goals. With practice, you can get quite adept at this. The more specific and detailed the pictures are that you communicate to the subconscious, is the more responsive and powerful the result.

Choose your own Beliefs

You can now choose your own beliefs and introduce them into your subconscious mind. Your present beliefs may have been put there by traditional experiences. The culture you were born into has had a powerful influence on your beliefs. So has your education and your circle of friends and family. You can now choose to reinforce those beliefs or to change them. That's your choice. You now have a choice to begin to program your subconscious mind for whatever you wish. Would you like to have a better job? Do you want to have better health? Start your own business? Travel to distant lands?

What should you expect as you begin to work with your subconscious mind? Don't expect to have everything handed to you on a silver (or gold) platter. This is not magic, although, in more ways than one it is a miracle. But there is still work to be done.

The first thing you should notice is a higher level of energy. You should have more creative ideas and a clearer vision of how you can achieve your goal. Flashes of insight. Courage and commitment to soldier on. Opportunities presenting themselves that you were not aware of before. Unexpected assistance from others. Confidence that you are achieving.

One popular, simple strategy to use the Alpha state to program the subconscious mind is the "A" card. The "A" stands for Affirmation. There was a time when I was struggling with self-confidence. The effect of this lack of confidence resulted in me avoiding situations and challenges that I faced, which only compounded my problem. So along with other strategies, I wrote on my "A" card (small 3 inch x 5 inch card) these words: "I am a confident, capable person". My "A" card was part of my dress, so it was always in my shirt pocket. I read it many times during the day and night. This meant that the message was repeated over and over again. Gradually my subconscious began to take notice. It began to change my behaviour, and make me more assertive and confident.

Your present beliefs are the result of experiences that you have entertained and repeated over and over again, until your subconscious now interprets them as your "truth."

How can you make all this work for you? Follow Darren as I take you through his growth experience. I feel proud to have contributed to it.

➢ Darren's Story

Darren was an average young man, growing up in what could be called a middle class environment in North America. His parents were not wealthy, but did their best to give him a good education. Darren however, was not an honour student and showed no enthusiasm for going on to University after graduating from school. His parents were troubled that he didn't seem to know what he wanted, resulting in some low paying service jobs that held no potential for his future development and maturity. Darren's father asked me to keep on eye on him, and if the opportunity arose, suggest some strategies to help him become more responsible and ambitious. When the opportunity presented itself I encouraged Darren to think of his successes. I complimented him on his achievements at soccer and other sports activities. I encouraged him to put his prized trophy, won at soccer, in a place where he could see it constantly. It would remind him of his success in that arena. The trophy would be his Affirmation. I wanted him to send a message to his subconscious that he was a champion. Later on we could make him a champion in other areas of his life. Right now we just needed to have him believe and "know" that he was a champion. Gradually I saw his confidence increase and his energy level rise.

Affirmations and Visualizations

Eventually, the time came to shift his focus to a career for the adult world he was about to enter. He seemed uncertain of the direction he should take, so we discussed what he liked doing. "What is your passion, Darren?" I asked. He seemed embarrassed to confess that he loved playing with computers. He described how fascinated he was with them and how he spent a lot of time on his computer, sometimes pulling it apart to discover just how it worked. I assured him that that was nothing to be ashamed of and suggested he might like to extend his education in that field. With a little encouragement from his Dad, he began a course on Computer Service – Network Technician. Because he was interested, he excelled at the Institute he attended and received his diploma. Darren continued to use affirmations and visualizations, as well as becoming an avid reader. Books by Maxwell Maltz,(*Psycho-Cybernetics*) Dr. Norman Vincent Peale (*The Power of Positive Thinking*) were his constant companions. His favourite was Claude Bristol's *The Magic of Believing*. He became more and more excited and enthusiastic with what he read, and shared with me that he would like to have his own business. I encouraged him to "reach for the stars", but reminded him he had to have a plan. I assured him he could achieve his dream if he only continued visualizing in detail what he wanted to do. We had some great discussions about The Subconscious Mind and how necessary it was to have it working for him.

It wasn't long before he was reading books and attending seminars on how to start and run a business. His enthusiasm was infectious and although his friends thought he had gone "over the deep end" their persistent ragging did not discourage him, but made him even more determined to prove them wrong.

I wouldn't like to give the impression that this was all a happy, positive thinking mind adventure for Darren. That everything just fell into his lap magically. Far from it! This was hard work. At times, frustrating work with lots of disappointments. But the important thing is that Darren achieved his goal. Because of all the visualizations and affirmations, he developed a belief and a commitment that he could do it. He worked his plan and achieved his goal.

Today, Darren is happy and satisfied with his achievements. For the past few years he has run a profitable and successful business servicing office computers. He was able to negotiate contracts with a few large corporations and continues to serve them. Darren's advice to his friends is that if he can do it, they can do it too.

Beliefs can perform miracles. The Greatest Teacher that ever lived said that if you have a small amount of belief (as small as a mustard seed) you will be able to move mountains.

Beliefs to Succeed

Wilma Rudolph "moved a mountain" with her beliefs. Let me tell you her story.

➢ Wilma's Story

Wilma was born in a small town in the southern United States. Her family was poor, and large. Very large! There were twenty-two children, and there was not much to pass around. To make matters worse, Wilma was a sickly child. Early in her life her illnesses left her with a deformed leg, the result of polio. The doctors said she would never walk, and questioned whether she would even survive under her challenging circumstances. Her mother would have none of that! She travelled to a neighbouring town to seek the services of an interested doctor, since in her own surroundings doctors were not quick to show interest in a poor black child.

Her newfound doctor gave some encouragement that perhaps Wilma might be able to walk, but it would need a lot of participation from the family to help. He suggested a treatment of massage for Wilma's legs. Mrs. Rudolph persuaded Wilma's sisters and brothers to help her massage Wilma's legs, and was encouraged when Wilma began to gain strength in her legs. The treatment continued and significant progress resulted.

By the time Wilma was fourteen she was walking and surprised everyone by showing interest in basketball. Soon she was running and shooting baskets. She became good enough to catch the eye of a well-known athletic trainer in that field. He became her mentor, and trainer, and soon she was running short distances and winning races.

In 1960 Wilma Rudolph, the girl who doctors said would never walk, found herself among the champion athletes preparing to go to the Rome

Olympics. She had come a long way! At that event Wilma became the first woman in the United States to win Gold medals in the 100 and 200-meter races as well as the 4 x 100 meter relay. A remarkable feat, especially since Wilma Rudolph had been declared to be a cripple for life.

How did Wilma Rudolph accomplish this incredible task? She never stopped believing that she could. She didn't just have positive thoughts about her success; she <u>knew</u> that she could succeed. She had a vivid picture of success in her mind and acted as if the picture was her present experience. Belief is not just positive thought, but a "knowing" that results in action. When we believe, we live and act as if we are already there. This is powerful stuff!

Our subconscious mind begins to call on all its resources to match the "knowing". If we need energy, the subconscious supplies energy. If we need courage, the subconscious supplies courage. If we need assistance from others, the subconscious attracts the assistance we need. This may take some time, but if we persist and maintain the belief state, the subconscious will bring into our environment the necessary tools to satisfy the need. Unfortunately we sometimes fail to maintain a believing attitude, and allow doubts and fears to interfere with work that our subconscious has already started.

➢ Peggy's Story

Peggy Jones is a girl I know. She believed she could be a great athlete. She had everything to encourage her to think she could be successful. She had an athletic build, she was healthy and loved the game of hockey. She talked about being a champion some day. But Peggy gave up on her dream. She stopped believing. She found a good excuse to stop training.

Truth was that she never really believed. Oh yes, she had positive thoughts. She even had pictures of the champions of her game on her bedroom walls. But she never had the most important picture, and never had it in the right place - the picture of herself winning the trophies and getting the applause, all vividly imagined in her subconscious mind. It never became a certainty for her. She never really "knew" that she was a champion.

Hope is not enough

Hope is good. We all need to have more of it. But hope alone is not enough to arouse the power of the subconscious mind to supply the elements that will take us to our dream. Positive thoughts are excellent, but they too are not enough to supply the determination, commitment and raw courage that we need. Only "acting as if the thing in question were real" will bring our dream into reality. William James, Harvard professor and America's best known psychologist said it best when he pronounced, **"we need only sincerely act as if the thing in question were real and it will infallibly end by growing into such a connection with our life that it will become real."** We need to "know" we are champions.

➢ The Amazing Medulla

As you read these words your heart is pumping. Without any conscious effort, it continues to pump. It may have been pumping for quite a while. Twenty years? Forty years? Fifty or sixty years? Doesn't matter, because you've never made a conscious effort to make it pump. Its all been done by your subconscious mind. A little part of your brain known as the Medulla, which is part of the brainstem has been working away for all those years. It also makes your lungs breathe, and your digestive system work. What a miracle!

The subconscious mind controls our health. There are thousands of other tasks being performed all the time. The subconscious is designed to keep our bodies in peak operating condition, and will do this as long as we don't use our conscious mind to thwart it. If we do, the subconscious will do all it can to correct the ill health if we instruct it correctly. If we send the right message to our subconscious mind it has all that it needs to return our bodies to perfect health.

The Placebo Effect

Dr. Bruce Lipton PhD suggests that the Placebo Effect should be a major topic of study in medical school. Dr. Lipton believes that medical education should train doctors to recognize the power of our "internal resources". Throughout his book, *The Biology of Belief* he describes the science of how thoughts control life. Dr. Bruce Lipton PhD is an internationally recognized cell biologist and University Professor.

Beliefs to Succeed

The Placebo Effect is the result of a patient taking "fake" medication, believing it will help, and getting better. The medication may be just a sugar pill, but has a result similar to a genuine medication. The conclusion is the patient's belief is the healing factor.

Norman Cousins found this out while he was critically ill, and used this knowledge to recover and tell the story of his discovery. Norman Cousins was a prolific writer, receiving over 50 honorary degrees and numerous awards during his lifetime. In his most successful book, *Anatomy of an Illness,* he described his recovery from one of his critical illnesses. In 1977 Cousins contracted cancer. He refused the standard medical treatment, and subscribed rather to a belief in laughter. He believed that laughter would release endorphins, which would heal him. He then proceeded to "laugh" himself to health. He obtained movies, read books, had people visit him who would make him laugh. He laughed until it hurt. His cancer went into remission. His experience was documented in his book, *Anatomy of an Illness*, which was later made into a CBS movie.

The Magnificent Healing Machine

In 1980 he repeated the experience when he suffered a near fatal heart attack. On arriving at the hospital he said, "Gentlemen, I want you to know that you're looking at the most magnificent healing machine to ever be at this hospital". He then set to work to prove that his subconscious was indeed the most magnificent healing machine. He recovered again by sending messages to his subconscious that laughter would heal.

Did Norman Cousins hypnotize himself and instruct his subconscious to believe he was healed? Did he use the Placebo Effect to regain his health? If he did, he would not have been the first to do so. There are hundreds of credible medical doctors, educators and psychologists that maintain that the Placebo Effect is alive and well.

One of the most dramatic and verifiable examples of the Placebo Effect and the power of belief took place in 1994 at the Baylor School of Medicine. It was reported in the New England Journal of Medicine in 2002. Dr Bruce Moseley was an Orthopaedic surgeon at the Baylor School of Medicine. He was disappointed with the surgery he was performing on patients with arthritis. Some patients improved, others did not. He made a radical decision to test a suspicion he had.

He operated on ten patients suffering from severe arthritic pain in their knees. Two of the patients had standard knee surgery in which the knee joint was scraped and rinsed. Three patients had a similar operation with just rinsing. No scraping. The remaining five patients had an operation, but nothing was done. Incisions were made, but neither scraping nor rinsing took place. Absolutely nothing. The incisions were then sewn up as if there had been surgery, but they were "fake" surgeries. All ten patients were told their procedures were successful and were given postoperative care complete with exercise program.

The results were shocking. The groups who received standard and semi-standard operations improved. But the Placebo group improved just as much as the other two groups. Their joints remained mobile and pain free for years after the "fake" surgery. Amazing! Absolutely amazing!!

The Placebo patients improved solely on the belief that they had experienced the procedure. They "knew" they had received the surgery and the "healing machine" (their subconscious mind) engaged and delivered.

The theme that runs through the story of Maxwell Maltz and self-hypnosis; through Norman Cousins and his laughter prescription; through Dr. Mosley and his "false surgery" is **Belief.**
Belief can kill, as some in the black arts can attest to. But belief can also open the door to a richer, fuller, healthier and happier life beyond our dreams.

9 Building Blocks to Beliefs to Succeed

- ➤ The Subconscious Mind
- ➤ The Gate Keeper
- ➤ The Self-Image
- ➤ The Alpha State
- ➤ Choose your own Beliefs
- ➤ Affirmations and Visualizations
- ➤ Hope is not enough
- ➤ The Placebo Effect
- ➤ The Magnificent Healing Machine

Chapter 3

MEANING AND PURPOSE

6 Building Blocks

When I was about ten years old, I got lost! My Father did not send out a search party and my Mother did not call the police. I had not wondered into the woods by myself, nor had I run away from home. Actually I was at home. I was in a room in my own house. But I was lost.

My Father was a hobby photographer. He liked to take pictures, but he also liked to process the film and produce his own black and white prints. To do this he had to have a dark room. In that dark room I experienced the most intense condition of darkness ever. There wasn't a glimmer of light while Dad was processing his films. The darkness was fearful.

> I got lost.

The day I got lost, my sister and I were in the room with him. He was busy doing his pictures, and after a while we got bored and wanted out. My sister tried to find the door but couldn't. She started to cry, so I tried to find the door to let her out. As I began to grope for the door in that awful darkness, I realized that I had no idea where I was. I was completely disoriented. For a moment I panicked and cried to my father, "Let me out Dad, I am lost." Then both my sister and I started crying.

After a few minutes Dad turned on the light, and suddenly everything changed. There was the door.

There were the windows. My sister and I were glad to escape from what for a moment had been a very distressing experience for us. It is not nice being lost.

The memory of that experience has come back to me many times during my life. During my teen-age years, I often felt fearful and apprehensive about the future. I felt as if I was in Dad's dark room again, and I had no idea where the door to the solution to my problems was. Unfortunately, because of teenage pride I didn't call out to Dad or Mom for help. In any case I felt they wouldn't understand. So I struggled through the best I could. Later on in adulthood, I found myself again in the dark room, without a clear path, still looking for the "door." What door? The door to happiness and peace of mind. Life seemed so confusing and at times pointless. Surely there was more to it than my boring job and small pay. Surely there was more than the daily grind and constant disappointments, and of course there was.

A Life of Purpose

It took me a while to find the "door", but eventually I did. You see, "The purpose of life . . . . is a life of purpose." Let me say that again with a little more emphasis, **"the purpose of life . . . . is a life of purpose"**.

Meaning and Purpose

Yes, without a purpose you are going to feel lost. And feeling lost means frustration, anger and hopelessness. This could lead to despair and disaster. But it doesn't need to. There is a way out. You can switch the light on and open the door. "The purpose of life . . . is a life of Purpose."

One of the best ways to describe the power and energy released by a personal Purpose is to show what happens when we focus the sun's rays. When you were in Kindergarten your teacher probably took you out one sunny day with a magnifying glass and some paper. As your teacher focused the sun's rays on the paper, smoke appeared, then fire, and in a short time the paper was consumed in flames. That's a good picture of what happens when you find your personal Purpose. The mind becomes focused, creative ideas begin to flow and you become consumed with the activities of the Purpose. Time is not a factor anymore and sometimes hours go by, seeming like mere minutes. When we find our Purpose we don't think of energy expended, as work. We never talk of our Purpose as a job. Rather we say, "I have a JOY". When we find our Purpose, we would work for free, of course if someone else would pay our bills. Work becomes a joy, and time goes by too fast. At last we have something that gets us up in the morning, puts a spring in our step and a smile on our face. "I'm just fine", you respond to your co-worker as she passes by, and you send her along with a cheerful "Have a nice day."

> ➢ A Mission Statement

All large business organizations and most small ones have a purpose, which they call a Mission Statement. A Mission Statement is a clear statement of an organization's reason for existence. What that does is to help members of the organization make good decisions and plans. The Mission Statement outlines a direction and provides a vision to help decision-making. For Instance, the Mission Statement for Disney World is: "To make people happy". Just a few words, but a clear statement of the purpose of the organization.

A Purpose or Personal Mission Statement as it is sometimes called, is much the same. It outlines a direction and provides a personal vision for your life. And just as in the case of a business, it helps in day-to-day decision-making, plans and goals. However, a Purpose is far more than a goal. Most people have goals, sometimes written down, sometimes not, but a Purpose goes further. Your Purpose is your philosophy of life, the "umbrella statement" under which your goals are constructed. Everything is affected by your Purpose.

In-Depth Reflection

How do you arrive at your Purpose? Try sincere, thoughtful, in-depth reflection. This is not a casual, incidental thinking exercise. My own experience in constructing my personal Mission Statement and Purpose was a demanding time. I still have the pages and pages of hand written notes as I struggled to arrive at a Purpose. My focus was on the legacy I wanted to leave, so my thoughts were, "what do I want people to say about me?" How do I want others to remember me? There was so much I wanted to do and be. I wanted to be respected and loved. I wanted to excel in my field of training. I wanted to be a good family member. I wanted to be useful. There were pages and pages of this! But now I had to reduce all this to just a few words, which would be my Purpose. Pages and pages of dreams boiled down to a Purpose. A few words, which would embrace and include all I had written. What a challenge!

> ➢ My Purpose

As I reviewed each page, I began to find a theme. I saw what my heart was trying to tell me. My Purpose became clear and my whole being responded with a joyous "YES". The theme was a need to help others. To inspire them to recognize the potential we all have as human beings. That they could be so much more than they thought they could be. I wanted to make others know that what had happened to me could also happen to them. That they could break down the mental barriers of fear and doubt and build confidence and hope and achievement. All this I put into three words. Three words that have inspired me, energized me, and translated my job into a Joy. And those words are:

Helping People Achieve

Doesn't sound like very much, does it? Just three simple words! What's all the hue and cry about?
Actually, you shouldn't be excited or impressed by those words. They aren't your words. Those words belong to me. They are the result of my search, my cry, my discovery. They are my Purpose.

Your Purpose

Go forth now, and find your own words. Make your own notes and experience your own struggle. Then review your pages of notes and find the theme, which will eventually become your Purpose. When you have done this and found your Purpose, you will find it to be one of the most stabilizing things in your life. You will know why you are here, and what you need to do. You will see the path you need to take, and you will possess oceans of energy and enthusiasm.

Here is the final step in arriving at your Purpose. Engage the power of belief to help you find your purpose. Tell yourself over and over again: "Congratulations! I now have a Personal Purpose. I am on the road to a new life. I will never be lost again, because the light has been turned on and I can see the door and all the windows. I have discovered a New World."

You must recall the words of William James, Harvard Professor, "we need only act as if the thing in question were real and it will infallibly end by growing into such a connection with your life that it will become real."

So congratulate yourself, and repeat over and over again, "I have found my purpose." Put it on your "A" card, but most importantly, implant it into your subconscious mind. It may take some time, but if you believe . . . change that to, if you "know" that you have a purpose, if you "know" that you are here for a reason, your subconscious will begin to show you what that is.

Meaning and Purpose

> The Big Picture

Your Purpose is the proverbial Big Picture! There will be many smaller pictures (goals), but there can only be one Big Picture at a time. The smaller pictures are the result of the Big Picture. There will be disappointments, interruptions and crises as you journey towards your Purpose. To cope with these challenges I have a story that may help you in the same way it has helped me.

> The story of Marcus and James

This story is about two brothers, Marcus and James. They were in the construction business and were often contracted for the building of small and large structures. One hot summer day they were erecting a wall in a building. Marcus is on one side, while James is on the other side, laying concrete blocks. It was hard work and they were sweaty and dirty. A friend drove up and stopped to talk with James. "How are you James?" he greeted. "How am I?" said James in a rather cross and surly tone, "I'll tell you how I am. I'm disgusted, frustrated and mad. I'm tired of this job. Look at my hands how filthy and grimy they are. Surely there has to be a better way to make a living." The friend empathized, and they talked about how hard life is and how other people seem to have all the luck.

Marcus recognized his friend's voice and called out from the other side of the wall. The friend walked around to say hello. "How are you, Marcus?" he greeted. "I'm just fine" said Marcus. "Life has been good to me. I am so glad to have a job that I enjoy. You know, sometimes the work is hard, and especially today with laying these blocks they are so hard on my hands, but I don't mind because I think of the Big Picture. You see, I never loose sight of what we are building here. We are building a Cathedral. People will come here one day with burdens hard to bear. They will sit in the Cathedral and listen to the great Pipe organ with its majestic music. They will hear the choir sing, and they will join with others in song and worship, and their burdens will be lighter. They will be thankful for a place of rest and inspiration. Yes, I never loose sight of the Big Picture. I am building a Cathedral."

As we go through life we tend to take our eyes off the Big Picture. So many things come in to attract our attention. Most of us get carried away with disappointments and problems and we begin to focus on them. We end up just like James, laying blocks and thinking how hard a job that is. We think only of our dirty hands and how difficult life is. Of course problems have to be attended to. A child cries and we have to go. A mother gets ill and we have to respond. Dad is in an accident and we have to lend support. But these interruptions should not make us lose sight of the Big Picture. Your Purpose is your "Cathedral" and although your hands will be dirty at times you need to focus constantly on the beauty and the wonder and the hope of "The Cathedral."

Make Things Happen

One of the first things you will notice when you have your Purpose is the new perspective you have on life. No more complaining and faultfinding. No

Meaning and Purpose

more misery and hopelessness. You will experience a certain satisfaction. You will begin to sense that rather than everything being in control of your day, you are now in control. You are calling the shots and you are making things happen. These are the first signs of Personal Leadership being born. You are in control of your life, and that has a dramatic effect on your behaviour. So much so that others will begin to notice. You will find a greater respect being afforded you and an appreciation of your opinion and advice.

That was one of the first things we noticed about Darren (Chap.2 P.34). He was in control. There was a sense of confidence that he had as he ran his own business. Although there were those who felt he couldn't succeed and told him so, he was firm in his resolve to make things happen. There were a few times when some plans did not work out, but Darren learned from his mistakes and soldiered on. The quality of Personal Leadership was evident.

Personal Leadership is knowing where you want to go. You have a clear vision of yourself and the future. You also have a clear picture of the challenges you face and a plan for coping with them. You are like an engineer preparing a blueprint for completing a project. Every length of lumber or steel is accounted for. Every screw and nail. You are very focused.

Personal Leadership prepares you for Public Leadership. Reaching for public leadership before you have acquired personal leadership is asking for disappointment. Public Leadership is winning the respect and admiration of others to the extent that they are willing to follow you. Public leadership without followers is pitiable. There is nothing as disheartening as someone trying to whip people into following, and thinking they are leading. True leaders inspire their followers and bring out the best in them.

As Darren progressed towards his goals, he began to get requests for Public Leadership. Some wanted to know his secret of success and how he was able to start his own business. Some wanted him to coach them. One of his proudest moments, he confessed to us, was being asked to be President for a community group. This was only the first request of many more. He was showing all the marks of Public Leadership. He had come a long way from those early days of confusion and uncertainty. He was now a confident leader. And it all started with setting goals and finding his Purpose. Darren is a good example of the transition and transformation from mediocrity to Purpose and Personal leadership and on to Public Leadership.

> Terry's Purpose

Another shining example of purpose was told in 1980 when a young man made a historic journey to fulfill his Purpose. 22-year-old Terry Fox journeyed to Newfoundland where he dipped his artificial leg into the Atlantic Ocean and vowed he wouldn't stop running until he reached Vancouver and the Pacific Ocean. Thousands of miles with only one leg. He called it the "Marathon of Hope."

Terry Fox had contracted cancer at a very young age. He was only 18 years old when he learned of a tumour in his right leg and his only hope was amputation. While recovering from this traumatic procedure, he saw suffering as he'd never seen it before. All around him in the cancer clinic he saw young boys and girls wasted by the disease and dying. He survived, but he left with a burden of

Meaning and Purpose

responsibility for what he had seen. His Purpose was formed in the pressure and the pain and the suffering of that clinic.

He purposed to earn One Million dollars for cancer research. He would call it "The Marathon of Hope". That Purpose drove him through the hills and highways of New Brunswick, across the farmlands of Quebec and into the towns and cities of Ontario. He touched the hearts of people of every province and they answered with millions of dollars. People wept as they watched him run. Finally, they named a mountain in his memory.

Some of us wondered as we watched him run through the hot summer days of August, through the wind and the rain, 23 miles every day, 143 days and 3,339 miles with just one leg. We wondered what was driving this young man. Where did the energy come from? The determination and the courage?

Always he took people back to the suffering and pain he had seen in the cancer clinic. "I was determined to take myself to the limit for those causes", he said. The power of a Purpose is not often seen as clearly and vividly as it was seen in Terry Fox's story.

The secret that not many were aware of was that what seemed like suffering and pain was actually a joy for Terry. Listen to him speak: "I loved it. I enjoyed myself so much and that was what other people couldn't realize . . . . People thought I was going through hell . . . . Even though it was so difficult, there was not another thing in the world I would have rather been doing." What a wonderful testimony for the power of a personal Purpose.

Transformation

Let me share with you my vision of where I know a Purpose can take you. It's a story told in Nature in all its wonder and beauty. It starts with a lowly worm, crawling along a leaf and feeding on it. The worm spins a cocoon and envelops itself completely. In just a few days time the lowly worm discards its cocoon, now transformed into a stunningly colourful and beautiful butterfly, which flies away on intricately patterned wings. A miracle of nature. A transformation from lowly worm to beautiful butterfly.

That is the kind of transformation that a Purpose and Vision can bring into your life. You may not want to be a Terry Fox. You may not even want to have your own business like Darren. But you do want to feel fulfilled and satisfied. You do want to know the reason you are here. You do want to find your Purpose.

> ➤ The Universe

In a previous chapter I mentioned that I was born with a curious mind. Along with millions and millions of fellow humans over the centuries, I too have looked up into the heavens and wondered. I too have tried to count the stars and wondered what is on the other side of the moon. I too have tried to imagine what creatures on other planets would look like, or if there was anything there at all. Mysteries, which I have wondered if we were even supposed to

Meaning and Purpose

wonder about. But maybe the biggest wonder of all, **Is there a Purpose behind all of this?**

Before we get to that, let's be clear about one thing. The Universe is not here by chance. There are some that would like to make us think that some time, somewhere, some how, life appeared by chance and luck, or some might say bad luck. That in a primordial soup billions of years ago, some amino acids and proteins came together and life appeared. That from this unlikely beginning, through eons and eons of time, this awesome complex body we live in was formed and developed by chance. That without guidance or design, you and I arrived with Consciousness intact in an environment perfectly suited to our needs. All by chance!

But not to fear. The chances of that happening are so infinitesimally small that it's not worth considering. The greatest and most respected minds down through the centuries have maintained that there was a Beginning. There is a veritable plethora of scientists, philosophers, theologians, prophets and sages who have declared that the Universe had a Designer. That God created!!

I am tempted to quote some of the great minds and thinkers that support a Great Designer. But I would rather ask you to look outside your window and take note of the miracles you see. The birds in flight, the trees in their summer glory, the little child playing on your street. Then ask yourself the question, did all these miracles happen by chance? I love one of Albert Einstein's quotes. I think it's his best. After all the accolades and praise as the greatest scientific genius, here's what he said, "There are two ways to live your life. One is as though nothing is a miracle; the other is as though everything is a miracle." Certainly his way was the latter.

So is there a Purpose for all of this? This finely engineered, exquisitely planned Universe. Planned to the degree that one tiny fraction of difference in its structure would cause it to fall apart. Listen to one of the world's most famous biologists, Dr. Robert Lanza: "Modern science cannot explain why the laws of physics are exactly balanced for animal life to exist. For example, if the big bang had been one-part-in-a-billion more powerful, it would have rushed out too fast for the galaxies to form and for life to begin. If the strong nuclear force were decreased by two percent, atomic nuclei wouldn't hold together. Hydrogen would be the only atom in the Universe. If the gravitational force were decreased, stars (including the sun) would not ignite. These are just three of more than 200 physical parameters within the solar system and Universe so exact that they cannot be random."

> The Theory of Everything

At this very moment the goal of the scientific community is trying to answer the question, "Is there a Purpose?" They have dug deep, looking for what is called The Theory of Everything. Their search has led them deep inside the atom that was thought to be the genesis of all matter. Surprise! Surprise!!

Turns out the atom is a world unto itself. Inside the atom are electrons, protons and neutrons. These subatomic parts are so small that in proportion the atom is as large as a football field, and the atom is something you cannot see with your naked eye.

They dug deeper and found that there is something smaller than these subatomic parts. They are called quarks. A quark is so small that our minds cannot conceive its size. It is beyond infinitesimal. Over in Geneva, Switzerland scientists are about to test a $5 Billion Hadron Collider atom smasher and hope to find something smaller than a quark. There seems to be no limit to how small subatomic parts are. Just as it seems there is no limit to how large the Universe is.

The Ultimate Purpose

I believe the purpose of the Universe is quite simple. It doesn't need an Einstein or a Darwin to tell us. If we pause and become quiet in our minds and our hearts, the answer comes. The Universe is specially designed and balanced for human beings to exist. It is the perfect school for us humans to make choices that can transform our lives to a higher consciousness. I believe that we all hear the call to reach for that higher consciousness but most of us ignore it. We prefer to wander on in the passions and pressures of our lower nature. We prefer to live by instinct. Jesus himself said, "Men loved darkness rather than light."

The rewards of "light" are what we all crave. At the deepest level of every human being that ever walked the earth is a longing, a craving, a deep desire for happiness, peace, joy and satisfaction. The wisest man who ever lived said, "light" brings a peace which passes all understanding.

6 Building Blocks to Meaning and Purpose

- ➤ A Life of Purpose
- ➤ In-Depth Reflection
- ➤ Your Purpose
- ➤ Make things Happen
- ➤ Transformation
- ➤ The Ultimate Purpose

Chapter 4

GRATITUDE THAT HEALS

7 Building Blocks

I picked up the phone and dialled her number.
 When she answered I said, "How are you Aunt Grace?" She laughed and said, "Vincent, how nice to hear from you. I was thinking about you and how I held you in my arms as a baby." Her voice was strong and clear. She recognized my voice immediately, before I told her who was calling. Not bad for a woman who just celebrated 102 years of a happy and healthy life.
 Aunt Grace is a bit of a miracle. She just laughs when I tell her that. She says she feels so thankful she can do the things she does every day. She is thankful for the home she lives in, for her health, for her daughters and her friends. She is just a bundle of thankfulness. Aunt Grace's life is full of gratitude. She has a strong enduring faith and a genuine love for everyone. Could this be the reason for her clear mind, cheerful attitude, good health and happy disposition at 102 years?

The Right Seeds

Happiness and Health are like flowers. They are the result of seeds planted in good ground. If the right seeds are in the soil and the right attention and care taken, the flowers of health and happiness will result. Seeds of Gratitude, Forgiveness, Patience and Love will grow you a happy and healthy life.

Many years ago, actually before I was born, Aunt Grace met my Father and Mother. They became fast friends. Since that time, she was known to us as Aunt Grace. As they lived together they learned the importance of patience and love and began to sow those seeds in their hearts. Dad and Mom are gone now, but Aunt Grace is still living proof of what Gratitude and Appreciation can produce. To me, along with everyone else in those long ago days, she always was Aunt Grace. She seemed to fit the role of an Aunt, because of her loving and appreciative attitude. She always made us feel so good, so important.

What Mom, Dad and Aunt Grace discovered, was a wonderful secret. They found out that behind all the mystery and miracles around them there is a Universal Power. They recognised and acknowledged that Power and a great peace and happiness began to manifest in their lives.

An Attitude of Gratitude

An Attitude of Gratitude is an acknowledgment that there is a vast and Infinite Power behind all we see, taste and touch. When we are thankful, we are expressing gratitude to a Power greater than ourselves. This Power is sometimes referred to as Universal Consciousness. When we express gratitude, we make contact with this Consciousness, which gives us peace and happiness.

To understand how Gratitude can impact your life, let's look at a typical day in Aunt Grace's life of 102 years. This day takes place many years ago, when I was still a young boy.

➢ Aunt Grace's story of a typical day

Aunt Grace is waking from a deep and restful sleep. She walks over to her window and looks out at an overcast sky. The temperature is just about one degree Celsius with about two centimetres of snow on the ground. She smiles and whispers "Thank you." She doesn't see the snow or the cold as a problem, but rather a miracle of nature. She is thinking of another beautiful day to live. Life feels so good to her as she prepares for the day's activities. She thinks of her good health, her home and her friends and whispers another "Thank you". Finally dressed she goes to her car. Problem! Her car does not start. She tries again. Nothing! She whispers a soft "Thank You" as she calls her Auto Association for help. She knows that everything happens for a reason. She is thankful there is a place to call. She will be late for work, so she makes the call and leaves a message that she will be there, but late. She is not stressed or worried.

When her Auto Association driver comes she showers him with thanks and appreciation for his help. The problem is incidental and she is soon on her way after a quick wave to her helper and a cheerful "have a beautiful day." At work she apologises to her manager and tells her how much she appreciates her patience. She says a big "thank you" to her work partner for filling in for her while she was late. At the coffee break she amuses the group with a story of how the Auto Association helper asked her to dinner. She stretches the story a little to lift the spirits of the group. Everyone has a good laugh and work seems a little less arduous. Aunt Grace is having fun, while spreading it around.

Gratitude and Happiness

Everyone loves a happy person. A happy person changes the dynamics in a room. Happiness cannot exist without gratitude. Most people speak of happiness as in the future. It is always out there beyond the horizon. "When I retire, when I win the lottery, when I get my vacation." But happiness is really a present condition. It is what we are. It is our state of mind, and those of us who practice grateful thinking find that happiness goes along with it.
Happy grateful people like to make other people feel important. That's who they are. Not to get something in return, not to sell them something or manipulate someone, but just because it is who they are.

> Mary Kay's Mission

It was said of Mary Kay, the woman who made millions from cosmetics that her mission was to make people feel important. Sure she made millions as a result, but as she herself said, "I wasn't that interested in the dollars and cents part of the business. My interest in starting Mary Kay Inc. was to offer women opportunities that didn't exist anywhere else."

I can think of people who use the power of gratitude for their own selfish gain. I meet them every day in stores, in malls, in offices and on the street. After a small purchase, I hear a memorized script, "Thank you, have a nice day." The words are right, but the warmth, sincerity and energy just isn't there. Somewhere they heard that those words would bring a customer back and would make them buy again. But true gratitude that inspires, carries the sounds of sincerity. It brings a smile and spontaneous gestures that tell you a person is engaging you and showing gratitude. It can't be imitated. The true product is easily recognized and accomplishes its objective of good feelings.

➢ Gratitude brings Serenity

Aunt Grace learned early in her life that Gratitude has many benefits. She is aware of a feeling of serenity and rest that it is bringing into her life. She wonders if her mental state and attitude is opening her to a higher influence. She is beginning to experience a new level of consciousness. She is calmer and more peaceful inwardly. She experiences a greater feeling of respect for others and her perception of love begins to change. She sees it as something more than physical and fleeting.

> **Gratitude is the Door**

She begins to see that Gratitude is a door that opens her heart and mind to Divine Consciousness. If this is so, she would like to have more of this serenity and peace. She expands and enlarges her Gratitude to include the mysteries and miracles around her: The privilege of life, the miracle of a flower, a baby being born, a song, the wind and the rain. She gives thanks for all this that she is a part of and privileged to experience. As her level of consciousness is raised, the level of her peace, satisfaction and rest is increased. As if the door to Divine Consciousness opens a little further to let in more peace and happiness.

The years go by and Aunt Grace becomes more and more confident that she is in contact with an unseen Force, bringing this Peace Rest and Happiness into her life.

She begins to notice something even more profound. Her health continues to be excellent despite her many years. Her doctor confesses his surprise that she is able to escape the normal health complaints of others at her age. He tells her that her internal organs are as strong and healthy as a woman twenty years younger. She knows now that Gratitude is the door that opens to Divine Consciousness.

Some scientific studies on Gratitude correlate very well with Aunt Grace's experiences. Robert Emmons PhD (University of California) and Michael McCullough PhD (University of Miami) in a long-term research project on Gratitude and its effect on health and happiness, discovered some interesting findings.

Grateful Thinking

Children who practice grateful thinking have more positive attitudes toward school and their families. Grateful people report higher levels of positive emotions, life satisfaction, vitality, optimism, lower levels of depression and stress.

Grateful people are more likely to acknowledge a belief in the interconnectedness of all life and a commitment to and responsibility to others.

In his book, ***Thanks! The new science of Gratitude,*** Dr. Edmonds says, "we discovered scientific proof that when people regularly engage in the systematic cultivation of gratitude, they experience a variety of measurable benefits: psychological, physical, and interpersonal."

Dr. Edmonds found that in carefully controlled tests, volunteers who maintained grateful thinking were far happier than others who did not. They exhibited more joy, more energy and more optimism.

What about a lack of gratitude? What happens when we are not thankful?

To understand how ingratitude can impact your life, let's look at a day in Egbert's life.

➢ Egbert's typical day.

Egbert is a person I know very well. Actually I have known him all my life. He is not as old as Aunt Grace, but the result of a life of ingratitude is already evident.

LIFE ONE-0-ONE Find your Purpose

Egbert did not sleep well, so he was less than pleasant as he awoke. Looking out on an overcast wintry day, his first comment was, "Not again!" He grumbles about harsh winters and boring jobs as he gets dressed for work. His head aches from his sleepless nights, and he resorts again to another aspirin. "Why does this have to happen to me?" he asks, and he resolves to see his doctor again. Egbert sees his life as a mountain of problems, and no solution in sight. He constantly complains and blames others. Nothing is ever right, and the future seems hopeless.

Ingratitude closes the door to Universal Consciousness, which results in a lack of serenity and peace. In the absence of these "flowers," the "thorns" of a lower consciousness begin to take root. Grief, regret, and sadness become evident. It is not long before further deterioration occurs leading to hopelessness and despair.

How does one escape from this cycle? How does one change ones perspective?

Try using your conscious mind to start a new program in the subconscious. Let me take you back to a story I told in Chapter 3. It is about Marcus and James. They were brothers and worked together at the same kind of work in construction. James saw his job as a hard and difficult experience while Marcus saw his (the very same job) as a joy. So it was all in their perspective. Marcus chose to see it one way and James chose to see it another. How strange! Could that happen to you? Happens everyday! The great majority of those around us see work and daily activities as unpleasant, difficult and boring, certainly not something to be grateful for. A few discover the joy of work and the peace and

Gratitude That Heals

satisfaction that flows from their gratitude for the opportunity.

I know that of which I speak. When I am in a workshop talking about the need for a positive attitude, I sometimes ask if there is anyone who gets up on a Monday morning and says, "Thank God it's Monday." The room of students usually breaks into loud laughter. What a foolish thing to say. Perish the thought of being thankful about another week of work. Rather think of the coming weekend five days away and say, "Thank God Friday is coming." How sad that so many spend their time, energy and life in work that does not satisfy, when a change in perspective would make such a difference.

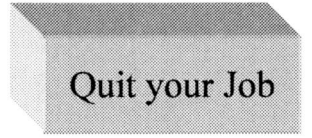

Quit your Job

You might wonder how this change might come about. Someone in a training session asked that very question one day. A young lady who we will call Gwen said, "Vince, you don't understand." They always say that. It's always someone else's fault. She continued, "If you had to work with the people I work with and with the boss I have, you would feel hopeless too. Sometimes I feel like quitting my job." I shocked her by suggesting that maybe that's exactly what she should do. She looked at me in stunned silence, so I continued. "Yes" I said, "Quit your job. On Friday afternoon, clean your desk and say to yourself, I am not coming back.

When you get home have a long talk with yourself. Tell yourself that on Monday morning you are going back to a new job, because you will have a new attitude. Write a list of all the positives you can be grateful for about your job. The first positive is you <u>have</u> a job. There are other positives, and if you look you will find them. Then make a list of the things you are going to change in your thinking. You will be more appreciative of others, you will be thankful for the company that provides you with the opportunity of a job, you will do your best at your job. By this time it will be Monday morning. Say out loud, "Thank God it's Monday." Put on your best dress and go out to your new job."

It is not easy changing your perspective. Your perspective is the result of the thoughts and actions over the past which your subconscious mind has accepted as true. So now you have the challenge of changing those "tapes" that are playing out in your mind. You have a job now as Chief Programmer. You will have to repeat, repeat, repeat the new message. That might be something like: "I am thankful for my new attitude of patience and hope". Make a few more and use them. It won't be easy. But think of the change that it will bring about in your life. From frustration and blame to happiness and appreciation. And you will be healthier too.

This is how Gratitude can be a benefit in your life. Use the power of belief to manifest the change in your behaviour. Summon all the sincerity you can muster to accompany your statements of gratitude. Feel it in your heart, express it in your voice if that's appropriate. Believe it deep in your inner self.

Gratitude That Heals

How would an attitude of gratitude affect your health? Why do happy appreciative people usually end up with excellent health?

Probably for the same reason that flowers that are fed with the right ingredients become more beautiful and exquisite than similar ones which have not had the same care. Why does fruit in a rich environment become more tasteful and nutritious than similar fruit that has not been cared for? Our subconscious mind is designed to keep us healthy and in peak condition. If we take good care of it we will achieve this objective. However, if we persist in introducing poisonous thoughts into our "healing machine" we will thwart the work it is trying to do.

One of the most powerful "poisons" that we tend to allow into our subconscious is fear. Fear is the father of doubt and insecurity. It tells our conscious mind that there is no hope of recovery. It plays that tape over and over in our conscious mind. The name of that condition is Worry. Again and again we tell ourselves, "I am ill and I am going to get worse." Eventually our subconscious is overwhelmed with the message and starts to work to make it so.

Of course there are other factors in the equation. Of course there are other aspects of our biology that affect our health. Certainly if we eat the wrong foods, our bodies will try to tell us. If we drink too much or smoke too much, or sleep too little and exercise too little and continually ignore the warnings and signals our bodies send us we will end up ill, regardless of our positive thoughts.

Another "poison" that we must expel from our conscious mind is unforgiveness. Of course that's only if we want to enjoy excellent health. Unforgiveness, anger and revenge will drag us down into a lower consciousness level where sickness and depression exist. Depression is a monster in our world today, destroying the lives of millions of people. How to convert this mighty ocean of discontent and despair before it becomes an all consuming fire or Armageddon will be the challenge for psychologists, psychiatrists and doctors.

A Gratitude Journal

Jack Canfield, one of America's great educators promotes the importance of a Gratitude Journal. He sees it as a valuable tool for development and growth. Take the time to list the things you are grateful for. Your health, your job and your friends. As you work on it you become more aware of the many things you need to be appreciative of. Try to be grateful for even the difficult and challenging situations. Begin to understand and appreciate how these situations lead to spiritual and emotional growth. Canfield says an Attitude of Gratitude will create a field of positive energy that will bring health and happiness into your experience.

Unfortunately, there are some people whose lives are so overwhelmed and cluttered with problems, crises and disaster, that suggesting a Gratitude Journal would be a shock to their system. And yet, those are the people that need it most. They are so burdened down with worry and hopelessness that they can't see a way out.

➢ The way out

The way out is to begin to focus on the good things in life and then they will see less of the problems. And that's where a Gratitude Journal can make a difference.

How do you start a Gratitude Journal? Grab a piece of blank paper and start writing. Did anything good happen to you today?

Did you have breakfast? "I am thankful I was able to have breakfast today."

Do you have a job or a business? "I am thankful I have a job/business to go to."

Are you reading this book? "I am thankful I can read."

Is there someone that loves you? "I am thankful that someone loves me"

Is your heart pumping and your lungs breathing? "I am thankful that my heart is still pumping and my lungs breathing."

    Everyday take a moment to write down five additional good things that you are grateful for. It may be challenging at the start, but soon you will enjoy the moments of focussing on the good things that are all around you: the flowers in your garden, the road you drive or walk on, the sky so blue, the snow, the rain, the birds that sing and on and on and on.

I'll close this chapter with some beautiful words by Sarah Breathnach in her book, *Simple Abundance:*

"As the months pass and you fill your journal with blessings, an inner shift in your reality will occur. Soon you will be delighted to discover how content and helpful you are feeling. As you focus on the abundance rather than on the lack in your life, you will be designing a wonderful new blueprint for the future. This sense of fulfillment is Gratitude at work, transforming your dreams into reality"

7 Building Blocks for Gratitude that Heals

- ➢ The Right Seeds
- ➢ An Attitude of Gratitude
- ➢ Gratitude and Happiness
- ➢ Gratitude is the Door
- ➢ Grateful Thinking
- ➢ Quit your Job
- ➢ A Gratitude Journal

Chapter 5

REACH FOR A HIGHER CONSCIOUSNESS

6 Building Blocks

Something stirred in the grass and made a sound.
    I moved over cautiously to see what it was. A baby bird was struggling to move. I moved closer and as it heard me it opened its mouth wide for food. I picked up this little miracle of nature and realized it was only a few days old. It had fallen from a nest in the tree and was weak and hungry. As I held the baby bird in my hand I realized that this frail, weak little creature represented a level of Intelligence and Wisdom. Perhaps it was not able to analyze and think as I could, but it certainly was aware of a presence that might satisfy its hunger.

    ➢ Dogs, Birds and Squirrels
I thought of all the beautiful birds that fly around our house. As I watch them I see their Intelligence being demonstrated. They are careful to watch for danger that could harm them. At the slightest sound or movement they are in flight. I began to think of other animals. The dogs next door, the cats that wander across our lawn, the squirrels and racoons. All these exhibit Intelligence. Wild animals in the forest, fish in the seas, polar bears in the Artic, and seals under the Artic. An awesome display of Intelligence surrounding us on every hand.

But it doesn't stop there! Cleve Backster discovered that the trees in our garden are aware of danger. Every flower, every tree, every blade of grass has a level of awareness and Intelligence. Cleve Backster is a polygraph expert. He operates equipment that indicates when a person is telling the truth or lying. This equipment is very sensitive and when connected to a human can pick up changes in the skin's electrical properties. These changes occur when a person tells a lie.

Backster attached the electrodes of a polygraph machine to the leaf of a plant in his office. He turned on the polygraph machine and got a response when he made a decision to harm the plant. He did not harm the plant. He just made a mental decision to hurt it, and the plant indicated on the chart paper that it was aware of his thought. The plant read his thought! Yes, the plant read his thought. Ridiculous? Insane? Balderdash? Backster has repeated his experiment over and over again in his laboratory. Other scientists too have confirmed that plant cells exhibit Intelligence.

> An Ocean of Intelligence

We are surrounded with Intelligence. It might be more correct to say that we are immersed in Intelligence. We are, along with the birds, and the squirrels and the trees, living in a great Ocean of Intelligence. An Intelligence and Wisdom that guides the planets in their orbits, brings the birds back from their annual winter homes and keeps our hearts beating and our lungs breathing.

This may or may not surprise you. For some people who lived thousands of years ago, this was common knowledge. They had always known that there was a Source from which Wisdom and

Intelligence flowed. The early pages of scripture are replete with the knowledge that the Creator was **"from everlasting to everlasting."** That meant for those of that day that there never was a time that Wisdom and Intelligence did not exist, and there never will be a time when It will cease to exist. They also knew that this Intelligence although invisible, was everywhere. They knew that It extended to the far reaches of the Universe. Indeed that It was Infinite and Eternal. Over three thousand years ago David, king of ancient Israel in one of his songs asks, "Whither shall I go from Thy Spirit?" He then acknowledges that "If I take the wings of the morning and dwell in the uttermost parts of the sea," You will still be there.

So what does all this mean, and how will it help us to be healthy and happy? How will it add meaning to our lives, and bring peace and satisfaction to our hearts?

> ➤ An Empty Mind

We are born with a clean and empty mind. We have no beliefs, no opinions, no prejudices, and no hatreds at birth. In the beginning we are just a blank slate, an un-programmed computer, waiting to run the programs of our choice. We are a little like the baby bird I picked up under the tree. We are instinctive creatures at birth. We cry for food and comfort, while the forces of nature work to make us grow. Soon, maybe too soon, we begin to exhibit more complex marks of our lower nature or consciousness. We exhibit selfishness and impatience, along with anger and aggression.

I remember as a little boy how angry I became when Mom or Dad advised me that I couldn't do something I wanted to do. The thoughts and emotions that welled up in me I am ashamed to even remember. Those youthful years were quite a struggle. I saw how my parents lived and could not understand their control and commitment to a Higher Consciousness. They tried to teach me that love and respect for others, forgiveness and acceptance was a better way. That didn't seem to make sense to me, especially when some boy at school was making my life miserable. My lower nature and consciousness was in control and pulling all my strings. I could hardly do anything different because I was out of control.

As I look around today, the great mass of mankind is where I was at that time. Out of control, influenced by their lower nature and consciousness with "tapes" of Fear, Insecurity, Pessimism, Anger, Revenge, Hate and Hopelessness playing in their minds. No wonder there are "wars and rumours of wars." No wonder we teeter on the edge of an abyss. No wonder the menace of nuclear disaster and planetary destruction threaten us all.

A New Heart

The greatest joy of my life is that I finally heard the voice of my Parents. Along with them I heard the constant "whispering" of a Higher Consciousness. The Universal Divine Consciousness that Aunt Grace spoke about during her 102 years of life began to influence me. I began to acknowledge that Consciousness and It began to influence my thoughts and actions. Peace began to flow into my life and a whole new paradigm was born.

This new life is of course what all the prophets of old have spoken of in the pages of scripture. Early prophets thousands of years ago experienced and taught the need for a "New Heart." This was confirmed and expanded on by the Greatest Teacher of all time, Jesus. One of the most beautiful stories told by Jesus was the story of a boy who lost his way and then found his Purpose.

➢ The boy who lost his way

This boy lived in a beautiful home with all the natural amenities. His parents loved him and tried to show him the wisdom of Higher Consciousness. But the boy's friends and his own lower nature finally influenced him. One day he said to his father, "Dad, my friends and I have decided to travel around the world. We want to see what's out there. Could you lend me some money for the trip?"

His father was not pleased and tried to persuade him to enjoy what he had at home. "Son, it's a harsh world out there full of danger." The boy was persistent and maintained, "I can take care of myself Dad. Don't worry about me. I'll be O.K.." And so he left home with all his friends.

Time went by and the father began to get reports that things were not going well. The boy along with his friends was living "riotously" with no respect for the standards of behaviour he had been taught at home. Finally, the boy became destitute and alone. All the money had been spent, his friends had gone away and he was left with nothing. Tired, depressed and afraid, he found himself washing dishes and cleaning floors in unfamiliar conditions. He was at the "end of the road."

A Blessing in Disguise

You might think of the "end of the road" as a disaster. In some respects it is. But for this boy, and many others who have reached that point in their lives, it can be a blessing in disguise. It was this experience that made this boy recognize the folly of his ways. It was this experience that made him commit to change his life direction. It was this experience that started him on a new path.

➢ A Transformation took place

He resolved to return home, and as he travelled a transformation began to take place. He began to see things differently. He got a new perspective and a new appreciation of the standards upheld at home. He remembered his father's patience, his kindness and his love. He began to see more clearly it was the better way. By the time he arrived home, he was a different boy. The boy that left home was proud, arrogant and selfish. The boy that came back was grateful, loving and kind. He had a New Heart.

A Control Shift

Paul, a student of Jesus, speaks in his letters of a transformation in our lives and an experience in which a new man/woman emerges. He speaks of this transformation as control being given over to a Universal Divine Consciousness. As a result of this control shift, the fruits of Divine Consciousness become evident. They are "love, joy, peace, longsuffering, gentleness, goodness, faith, meekness, temperance"

> Scattered across the World

There are those who have heard and responded to the influence of Universal Divine Consciousness in every land. Most go about their lives silently and quietly, but at times there emerges in public view an outstanding example of Higher Consciousness. Mother Theresa was a shining example of Love, Compassion and Kindness. Mahatma Gandhi refused to allow his lower nature and consciousness to control him even in the face of brutal and cruel treatment at the hand of his oppressors.

One of the most admired leaders today, revered in every country and honoured by everyone as he received the Nobel Peace Prize for his leadership in South Africa, is Nelson Mandela. He is a shining example of Forgiveness, Patience and Love. Were he to have followed his lower nature, he would have sought revenge for all the years he spent in prison, fighting for a just cause. Instead, he forgave the leaders of Apartheid and became an Icon, a name for the Ages.

There is a sequel to the story of the boy who lost his way. He had an elder brother who stayed at home. He was a good boy, but there was something he still needed to learn. He needed to learn compassion and forgiveness.

Compassion and Forgiveness

When his younger brother came back from the far country, the father prepared a great celebration. "My son that was dead is alive again, he was lost and is found." The father was filled with joy and arranged a feast to welcome his son home. But the elder brother was incensed. He refused to attend the feast and went off in a huff. He said it wasn't fair, and he would not forgive his brother. He ignored his father's pleading and wallowed in his anger and his wrath. He became very bitter.

Our nature would like to make us think that we hurt others more when we refuse to forgive. Experience teaches that we hurt ourselves far more. I have watched some choose blame and bitterness when others have hurt them. I have watched them allow negativity to consume their days, and as time went on drag them down into frustration, despair and sadness.

When we allow bitterness and anger to control our lives, we begin to close the door to Higher Consciousness. We shut out the "light" and the peace, joy and happiness that come with it. We give power to our lower nature, which blinds our eyes to all that is good and right around us. We begin to see only the things that are wrong. We see only the darkness.

> ➤ It shall be in you

Years ago my wife and I travelled through the heart of Europe. It is a journey that I will never forget.

What magnificent buildings. The architecture going back through many centuries. I remember some of the cathedrals we visited with their towering steeples and spires. Inside these awesome structures there seemed to be an atmosphere of wonder and mystery. Everything seemed designed to suggest that this is where you will find God. This is the place to find Divine Intelligence.

But this is an illusion! Divine Intelligence is everywhere. In the cathedrals yes, but also in the schools and in the homes and in the business offices of every land. But much more important, Divine Intelligence is within us. The Bible teaches, "It shall be in you." Over and over again in letters to the early Christians, Paul reminds them that, "we are the temple of the living God."

The Relaxation Response

Years ago I read Dr. Herbert Benson's book, *"The Relaxation Response"*. My motive in reading it was to find an answer for a condition of stress and worry, that I was experiencing. Dr. Benson's book promised relief from stress and an improvement in health. The Relaxation Response is a technique for calming the mind. The objective is to stop the wild, uncontrolled thought patterns, which cause sleepless nights and tired days. I learned from Dr. Benson's book that 80% of our illnesses develop because of stress.

After a few months of the technique I became a much calmer person. I had greater control over my thoughts and stopped worrying. I began to give less attention to my problems and more attention to my achievements. I became more of an optimist and less of a pessimist.

The technique taught me how to be quiet inwardly, and become more calm and reflective. It was in these moments that the "whisper" of Divine Intelligence seemed more pronounced. It was in these moments that feelings of Peace and Love, Hope and Caring appeared. In time my moments with the Relaxation Response was more for the benefit of spiritual health than for physical health.

Meditation

Of course, the Relaxation Response has been around for a long time. Earlier generations called it Meditation, and people were encouraged to use it to become more aware of a Higher Consciousness. The Bible is filled with references to Meditation. More recently, the emphasis has been on physical health, but meditation is still one of the routes to Universal Divine Consciousness

Dr. Benson describes the process as quite simple. Find a quiet environment where you can be alone with no distractions. Find a quiet room in your home, your school, your office, or maybe your car (parked!).

➤ The Process

Assume a comfortable position. Sitting in a comfortable chair is best. Do not lie down as this usually results in falling asleep.

Empty your mind of all its activity. Try to stop the persistent, uncontrolled thought process. To aid in this respect some recommend that you focus on your breathing, concentrating on each breath, inhaling and exhaling slowly. Some suggest a word or phrase ("I am thankful"), which you repeat over and over. Last but not least, be kind to yourself. Distracting thoughts are difficult to eliminate. Be patient, and just let them happen, but bring your attention back to your point of focus. With time you will begin to control your random thought activity and experience an inner peace and calm. In time you will appreciate the positive thoughts of love, forgiveness and peace that will flow into your heart and mind. There is so much more about meditation and its benefits in the libraries and bookstores of the world.

6 Building Blocks to Higher Consciousness

- ➤ A New Heart
- ➤ A Blessing in disguise
- ➤ A Control Shift
- ➤ Compassion and Forgiveness
- ➤ The Relaxation Response
- ➤ Meditation

Chapter 6

LOVE, JOY AND PEACE

7 Building Blocks

He watched her as she walked slowly towards him.

She was a vision of beauty. A flower in its brightest bloom. A ray of sunlight shining into his heart and making him proud. She was his bride, and this was their wedding day.

As he watched her come towards him in her enchanting white dress with its flowing train, he thought of all the times they had talked about this day. He remembered how they had laughed and cried about their future life together. And now that their wedding day had come, he remembered how they had talked about love. He remembered how she said that the day would come when the beauty he so admired would fade away. He remembered she told him that one day she would be old and wrinkled and grey, and he remembered how she looked into his eyes and said, "what then? Will you still love me?"

And he remembered how he told her that his love would never die. He told her his love was never about her outward beauty, but that from the very day he met her he always loved her inner beauty. He told her as their friendship grew how safe he felt with her. How easy it was for him to open his heart and his soul and share it with her. He told her how much he trusted her and knew that she would never knowingly hurt him. All this he remembered as she walked towards him on their wedding day.

The love that brings happiness into our lives is more than physical attraction. Nothing wrong with physical attraction, but when we substitute it for love we sell ourselves short. We also set ourselves up for disappointment and regret. Love that will endure goes deeper; far, far deeper. It is called unconditional love and it does not apply only to marriage. It applies to all of life.

If we live our lives and never experience unconditional love, we die unfulfilled. We have missed the road. Somewhere along the Highway of life we got side tracked. Maybe as we were travelling we came to a sign that said Anger, and we followed that sign. Maybe another sign said Jealousy, and we followed that one. Those of us that have been down those roads know of the tragedy they lead to. Yes, we can tell you about disappointment and despair, about the cancer of unforgiveness and revenge. But we can also tell you about "coming to an end of ourselves." About the long road back to the Highway and getting a new heart and a new life.

Unconditional Love

Sometimes we find ourselves in a quandary about unconditional love. We wonder what it really is. It is really not too hard to understand. There is Conditional love and there is Unconditional love.

When we love conditionally it means there are conditions. "I will love you if you do as I say. I will love you if you do what I want. I will love you if you love me." There are always conditions. There is always a price to pay when we love conditionally.

When we love unconditionally there is no price. There is no condition. There is no expectation of a reward. I spoke to a woman this morning who is a good example of unconditional love. She has a son who loves her and cares about her in her old age. He himself is not that well, but goes to great lengths to answer her calls and meet her needs. She loves him dearly. You would too.

She has another son who has given her nothing but pain and distress. His life has been a disaster with broken marriages and lost jobs. He calls on her for help even in her old age. Nevertheless, she loves him dearly. Would you? There are no conditions to her love. She would not even think of it.

Conditional love brings constant disappointment and sadness into our lives. Witness the broken homes and shattered lives in our world today, because one partner did not pay the price the other expected. Some have referred to conditional love as an "imitation of the real thing" and sadly, many have never recognized the counterfeit.

Unconditional love cares about others no matter what. That does not mean that we agree with their mistakes and blunders. We acknowledge their failures, and if appropriate try to help directly or indirectly. But there never is any doubt about our love for that person. That means that even if someone hurts us we still love them, which takes us back to some words by the Great Teacher Jesus: "Love your enemies, bless them that curse you, do good to them that hate you . . ."

Unconditional love does not mean hugging and kissing your enemies. That's not necessary. But it does mean having a healthy respect for a fellow human being. Courtesy, Kindness and Consideration are very much in order.

➢ Nothing more important

Paul a follower of Jesus, in one of his letters, gave us a beautiful picture of unconditional love. He prefaced it by suggesting that there was nothing more important. He said if you had all the wealth, all the knowledge and all the power, but did not have love, you were a loser. He then went on to describe love:

> "Love is patient, love is kind.
> It does not envy, it does not boast,
> It is not proud. It is not rude,
> It is not self-seeking,
> It is not easily angered,
> It keeps no record of wrongs.
> Love does not delight in evil
> But rejoices with the truth.
> It always protects, always trusts,
> Always hopes, always perseveres.

Love Yourself

Of course unconditional love also relates to ourselves. There can be no love, either conditional or unconditional without first loving ourselves. This makes a lot of people very uncomfortable. This is when words like Pride, Conceit and Arrogance come to mind. We don't want to be any of these negative things, and we don't need to be. We can still love ourselves and avoid Pride, Conceit and Arrogance.

Love begins with us. When we love ourselves we begin to experience what love is, and we can share it with others. Conversely, when we hate ourselves we begin to share it with others. We condemn and blame ourselves and end up condemning and blaming others.

I know a woman named Gwen, and you probably know her too. You met her at work, or maybe at church or at your community meeting. Gwen did not do well at relationships, and is now lonely and aloof. She does not like herself. She carries guilt and blame on her shoulders and it weakens her. She looks out from under the weight of distress and sadness in her life and sees a world of deception and hypocrisy. It structures her paradigm of an unjust Universe without meaning or purpose. She looks around for someone or something to blame, and never suspects that it all might have started with her. She never realizes that all this sadness is what she attracted to herself. The law of attraction in action again!

Forgive Yourself

Unconditional love also means that we forgive ourselves. Some of us find it hard to forgive

Love, Joy and Peace

ourselves. We nurture blame and shame and drown ourselves in despair. We allow the millstones of self-doubt to keep us mired in failure. If there is one thing that scripture teaches us, it is that we are forgiven. If there was no forgiveness, there never would have been a David to write the Psalms. Nor would there have been a Paul to write his letters. Both men strayed from the Highway and could have stayed in the morass of their mistakes, but rose up, forgave themselves and became servants and instruments for good in their day.

> ➢ The Wedding

Remember the wedding? Let's go back there.
She is still walking but a little closer now. She sees him standing there waiting for her. She remembers the first day they met. It seems such a long time ago. So much has happened. It seems like a lifetime ago they kissed for the first time, and he told her he would love to marry her. He had been so respectful. He was conscious and caring of all her fears while mindful of the gravity of such a decision. It had to be for life. It had to be "until death do us part." He was so patient and considerate and understood. She had learned to trust him and then she learned to love him, unconditionally. She thought of the words she had asked to be included in the ceremony. They were her favourite words about love. A wise man named Solomon had written them thousands of years before. "Many waters cannot quench love, neither can the floods drown it." They had talked about those words and they had promised each other that together they would face the floods and they would overcome. They knew that there would be floods but they had a strong commitment. She felt safe. She reached where he stood, and he held

out his hand. She took it, and started a new life with him.

I found this quote by Dr. Elizabeth Kubler-Ross. I hope you like it as much as I do.

> If we make our goal to live a life of compassion and unconditional love, then the world will indeed become a garden where all kinds of flowers can bloom and grow.
> - Dr. Elisabeth Kübler-Ross,
> Late Author of *On Death and Dying*

One of the flowers that blooms and grows as we practice unconditional love is Joy. It is a flower that we all want to have in our garden.

➢ Helen's Joy

Just this week I was at a Toastmasters meeting and Helen, a member, was giving a speech. She talked about music and then told us of an experience she had. She was walking in the subway station when she heard strains of music in the distance. As she drew nearer the music became more and more compelling and as she reached the performer the music filled the whole area. The high ceiling and bare walls of the building acted like a cathedral to swell the sound. The beautiful strains of the violin reverberated through the building and overwhelmed her. It consumed her. It seemed to her as if the music had invaded her soul and thrilled her entire being. Tears rolled down her cheeks as she became enthralled and experienced rapture. This was her moment of joy.

Most of us have experienced moments of joy. We have watched the sun go down in a cloud of glorious colour. We have walked in the woods on a Fall evening, surrounded with every shade of green and gold. Precious beautiful moments that stirred our hearts and brought tears to our eyes. But for most us, these moments are too few and too far between. We wonder if we can experience this joy always. If it can become a way of life for us. But sadly, we settle for fun. We substitute fun for joy and happiness. Again we sell ourselves short.

> Fun is not Joy.

Fun is a temporary thing. Fun is winning a ball game. Fun is enjoying a nice lunch. Fun is playing a practical joke on a friend. Fun is all right in its place, but joy is far deeper. Joy is a soul experience. Its energy pervades our whole being. At that level we know that life has meaning and purpose and we are satisfied that we are part of the meaning and purpose.

Give Yourself Away

Joy comes when we give ourselves away, and let go our ego. Joy comes when we forget ourselves in the pursuit of our purpose. Joy comes to a Terry Fox, pounding his artificial leg on the hard pavement of twenty-three miles of highway every day, lost in his dream of running to save others. Joy comes to a Mother Teresa tending the sick and dying, in the indescribably poor circumstances they lived in, but thinking only of their welfare. Joy comes to you and

I in our daily tasks, seeing the big picture and forgetting the aches and pains and pressures that we all must experience. Joy comes to you and me when we love unconditionally, forgetting the little faults and failures of those around us.

The most joyous person I know is Aunt Grace who I talked about in Chapter 3. She exudes joy with her laughter and gratitude. Amazing! after so many years of life's challenging tests and trials. Most people at her age of 102 years are tired and weary and eager to go home. But Aunt Grace gives the impression she is just getting ready to start.

Of course she is aware her time now is short and she will soon be gone, but she is enjoying the moments that are left. What drives her? What energizes her? If you asked her she would say, "I have a deep faith and Trust that I am safe and everything will be taken care of." Sounds a little like one of the most famous psalms of David: ". . . Though I walk through the valley of the shadow of death I will fear no evil, Thy rod and Thy staff they comfort me."

Prescription for Joy

An abiding faith in something greater than ourselves is a prescription for Joy. Down through the ages, multitudes have proven this in their own lives. Doubts, fears and disbelief have brought only disappointment and a sense of emptiness and lack of purpose. Faith, belief and commitment have been the harbingers of Joy, song and laughter in life. Find a cause, commit to a purpose, give yourself away and enjoy the satisfaction you were meant to experience.

Laughter

Laughter can encourage Joy. Laughter may not be true Joy, but it will encourage the development of Joy. More and more the benefits of laughter are being discovered through research. A Jamaican friend of mine was discussing these benefits, and shared this experience.

➢ Laughter experience

Mark went to a psychiatrist with a problem. "Every time I go to bed I think there is somebody under my bed. I'm so scared. I think I'm going crazy."
"Not to worry" said the psychiatrist, "just put yourself in my hands for one year. Come and talk to me three times a week, and we should be able to get rid of those fears." "How much do you charge?" Eighty dollars per visit, replied the doctor. "I'll think about it," said Mark.

Six months later the doctor met Mark on the street. "Why didn't you ever come to see me about those fears you were having?" he asked. "Well" said Mark, "Eighty bucks a visit three times a week for a year is an awful lot of money. I met this Jamaican guy and I told him about my fear, and he said no problem man, just give me $50 and a dozen Red

Stripe Beers and I'll tell you what to do. He cured me. I was so happy to have saved all that money that I went and bought me a new car." "Is that so! And how may I ask did the Jamaican cure you?" "He told me to cut the legs off the bed! Ain't nobody gonna go under my bed now!!"

We had a good laugh about that one. Actually, we both felt good after, as if we had a good massage. According to research, laughter reduces the level of stress hormones like cortisol, adrenaline and dopamine. It also increases the level of health-enhancing hormones like endorphins and neurotransmitters. All the more reason why we should laugh more. Recognizing the benefits of laughter, there has been an increase in the number of laughter clinics and clubs. There is even a laughter yoga. As we lighten up and laugh more, we find that we take ourselves less seriously as we recognize there is something so much greater than ourselves.

➢ The search for Peace

The United Nations (UN) is an international organization whose stated aims are to facilitate cooperation in international law, international security, economic development, social progress, human rights and achieving world peace. The UN was founded in 1945 after World War 2 to replace the League of Nations, to stop wars between countries and to provide a platform for dialogue.

Two thousand years after the birth of the Prince of Peace, we are still searching for peace. It seems that we still do not yet understand the prescription for peace. We continue to search through the logical avenues such as the League of Nations and the

United Nations. But evidently the answer is not there. Maybe the answer is somewhere else.

> Shangri-La

Long ago I read a story about Shangri-La. Shangri-La was a far away place, where trouble and worry were left behind. A land where there was harmony and peace, and where men and women were almost immortal.

Shangri-La was a fantasyland. In the novel *Lost Horizon* by James Hilton, it was a mystical, magical valley hidden away in the mountains of Tibet. It was a permanently happy and peaceful place where men and women slowly aged as the centuries passed. Shangri-La was a land of hope and promise. Its purpose was to be a haven when our sad world had consumed itself in destruction and chaos.

James Hilton created this fantasyland to compare with his experience, and our own experience today. All around him was the antithesis of Shangri-La. He saw wars and rumours of wars. He saw greed and dishonesty rewarded. He saw violence and outrage and man's inhumanity to man. And as in Hilton's day, and in our own time, we wonder if there is a Shangri-La that we can escape to. A place where there is harmony and peace. A place where there is hope for a better future.

> The good news

The good news is that there is such a place. Not necessarily in the far flung mountains of Tibet, nor in the lush, luxuriant vegetation of Hawaii or the warm waters of the blue Caribbean, but right here within you and within me. The message that has come down through the centuries is as true now as it was then: "The water that I shall give him shall be *in* him, a well of water springing up into everlasting life." The promise is that we can experience a peace, which passes all understanding. Despite all the turmoil and distress, we can experience a serenity and peace in our own personal Shangri-La.

Shangri-La within

We can find this Shangri-la within ourselves. We start by learning how to control our thoughts. Most of us are controlled *by* our thoughts. We make no effort to choose the thoughts that lift us up to a higher level. Our mind then becomes an unattended garden. Weeds of jealousy, anxiety and fear begin to grow, and in time take over and control our mind.

We must exercise our greatest gift of choice, and begin to plant seeds of respect and love. In time, and with consistent attention they will grow and become a positive attitude. We develop a "habit of thought" and we are on our way to our Shangri-la.

Our next step will be to establish our purpose. A life without purpose is like a ship without a rudder. It sails in any direction the wind is blowing. Life becomes a meaningless ritual of pointless activities with no clear objective. A purpose gives meaning to the daily tasks and demands of life. We see the Big Picture and how the little pieces fit together. We are building towards our Shangri-la.

In time we begin to see the ultimate purpose. That is, our place in the Universe, the need for a new heart, and the development of a Higher Consciousness. We begin to see that our life matters in the great scheme of things. That there is a plan and a reason for all that we see around us. We realize that a Great Designer put us here and is taking care of us. As we surrender ourselves to the call of Higher Consciousness, a great peace comes into our lives. We know that nothing can harm us because we are part of an everlasting plan. This faith and belief in a Higher Power brings serenity, peace and hope to our souls. When this serenity and peace exists in our hearts and in our souls, it will spread and flow like a great wave and bring peace to our world.

One of the most beautiful illustrations of Peace was given by my minister in a Sunday morning meeting when I was a little boy. I never forgot it. It is indelibly impressed on my mind. It comforts me in time of stress and distress. It supports me when I feel overwhelmed with the events of the day. It gives me hope that everything is going to be all right.

> Sunday morning sermon on Peace

"The story of peace is a beautiful story of an artist who was seconded to paint a picture of peace for a famous gallery. The artist struggled with the picture that he should put on canvas to fitly convey the value of life's greatest treasure. He pondered over the vision of "the leopard lying down with the kid"; the miracle of a new born babe in it's mother's arms; the golden leaves of a Fall evening, as the Sun spread its dying light in the sky. But none of these seemed to satisfy his struggling mind.

Then the thought of a little bird in her nest seemed to give him some rest. But not just a bird in her nest; not just the vital, fluttering wings and feathers now at rest. But a bird in the midst of the fury of a tempest, serene and calm on her nest in the cleft of the rock above the raging sea. A bird at peace in the knowledge that she was safe. And so he painted the tempest. An angry sea! Waves breaking against a towering cliff. The white water receding as another mighty wave with its roar and power crashing against the immovable wall of rock and stone. The sound of pounding surf could almost be heard as his vision was revealed on the canvas. And then with a satisfied smile, he quietly placed in the top of the impenetrable rock, a little bird sitting on her nest. High up above the roar of the tempest, beyond the scream of the tumultuous wind raging between the crevices of the rock, he made her look down on the tempest below with calm and confident gaze. She was at peace and at rest in the knowledge that she was protected and safe, in a place where nothing could harm her. Not the wind, not the rain, not the roaring sea, not the tempestuous wind would ever reach that quiet spot in the cleft of the rock."

7 Building Blocks to Love, Joy and Peace

- ➤ Unconditional Love
- ➤ Love yourself
- ➤ Forgive Yourself
- ➤ Give yourself Away
- ➤ Prescription for Joy
- ➤ Laughter
- ➤ Shangri-La Within

Chapter 7

THE BEGINNING

"What happens when we die?"

The question startled me. I wasn't ready for it. I was leading a training workshop on customer service, but as quite often happened, we had wandered far off topic. There was silence in the room. Finally I said, "Does anyone have something to tell us that might help?"

A young woman spoke up quietly and reluctantly and said she had an experience, but she didn't like to speak about it. She said some had laughed at her and ridiculed her story. I assured her we would respect her experience. After she told her story, I was so impressed and inspired that I asked her to write out what she had said, so I could have it for my records. This is what she wrote:

➢ Laura's Story

"The birth of my first child was an experience I will never forget. Not only for the obvious reasons but also at this time I encountered a near death experience (NDE). The date was Nov. 9, 1983. Due to complications during childbirth an emergency caesarean section was scheduled. During the surgery I was under a general anaesthetic and something amazing happened. Something I can recall vividly and I shall never forget.

All of a sudden I could feel myself being lifted out of my body and I was looking down at

The Beginning

the surgery table with the doctor and nurses around me. The next thing I remember I looked up and saw this bright white light and a tunnel leading up. I followed this light up into the tunnel and at the end of the tunnel I could see both my grandparents and sister who had passed away years ago. I can't recall any words spoken as I was drifting upward towards my deceased members of my family. I could see their faces so clearly as they were watching me come towards them. I felt excitement seeing them again, the same feeling anyone would feel not seeing somebody they loved for a long period of time. This light was so intense and beautiful, nothing like I have ever seen on earth. I felt at such peace with myself without any fear whatsoever. I kept floating upward almost to the end of the tunnel when I could see beyond. It was a beautiful place. I think what I saw was heaven. I was almost face to face with my sister when I suddenly turned back. At this point I woke up in the recovery room.

I believe the reason I came back was because I was needed here on earth due to the birth of my daughter and it was not my time to go. A few hours later I was taken back to my room when almost in a panic state I recalled my experience to my immediate members of my family. The reaction I got was disbelief except for my father who believed everything I was saying. Both my husband and my mother shrugged it off as a dream I had. In reality people do not dream while under anaesthetic. Later I asked the surgeon if everything went OK and he confirmed everything went well. I cannot explain what happened but I know it happened and it doesn't matter to me who believes me or not. One day their turn will come and I am sure they will have the same experience.

They say people who have NDEs always come back with a message. My message is there is nothing to be frightened of when death is approaching. Death is a beautiful part of life. One day you will be reunited with the people who have passed before you. Since this experience I have felt an inner peace with myself and my fear of dying is no longer. There are days when I can't wait to have this experience again because I know I will see my sister again."

Try to imagine the reaction of other students when Laura had finished her story. You could have heard a pin drop. Laura herself was crying quietly in her chair. I said "Thank you Laura for sharing your story with us." That night I read her story over and over again. I found a great joy filling my heart. I felt like shouting and singing. I was overwhelmed with the implication that we do not die. That Consciousness survives death. There is life after life. Death is the beginning of something far greater and more magnificent than we can ever imagine. The grave is not the end.

If Laura were the only one to tell of Consciousness surviving death, I would probably have second thoughts. However, I soon learned that Laura's story was not unique. I discovered that literally thousands of people had a similar experience. Actually, in a poll taken by Gallup in 1982, eight million people in America acknowledged

The Beginning

they had an experience where their consciousness left their natural body. They experienced another dimension.

Hundreds of books have been written about NDEs. I had the opportunity of meeting the most famous author on the subject of NDEs. I attended a seminar by Dr. Raymond Moody, who authored *"Life after Life"*, one of the first and one of the best books on the subject. I found Dr. Moody to be a kind, sensitive and thoughtful man, who presented the case of life after life in easily understood terms. Dr. Moody himself had not experienced an NDE, but he had interviewed thousands who had the experience.

Dr. Moody, after interviewing thousands of people who have experienced a near death experience, says that most people report the same sequence of events. This sequence is repeated across all cultures, countries and races. It doesn't matter where they lived or who they were; the experience was the same. Amazingly, children at very young ages experience NDEs and report much the same sequence of events also. On his website, Dr. Melvin Morse tells the story of an eight year old child who was resuscitated after his heart stopped beating as a result of kidney failure. The child's first words were: "Dr. Morse, I have a wonderful secret to tell you. I was climbing a staircase to heaven." Dr. Morse is a paediatrician and neuroscientist who has been researching NDEs in children since 1980.

➢ Two significant phases.

The sequence of events, which Dr. Moody reports, has two very interesting and significant phases. The first phase occurs after the patient's consciousness has separated from their body and they find themselves in another dimension. They have died.

This phase is referred to as a Life Review. Patients find it very hard to describe a life review. It takes place in an entirely different dimension with apparently different laws. They say that they see their lives played out before them in detail, with every thought, action and experience all at the same time. During the review, time is not a factor. All of life is reviewed in what seems like a few seconds. As they view their lives as observers, they are also in the review. They see and feel how their actions affected others. They actually feel the pain they caused in some situations. They also feel the love and warmth resulting from actions of kindness and compassion. Patients report that the review is not a judgement or criticism, but rather a report on how they lived their lives. The whole review process seems to be designed to stress the need for learning and living acts of love, compassion and kindness.

➢ After the NDE

The second significant phase is what happens to patients after their near death experience. As they recover from their illness and return to a normal life, their lives are changed profoundly. They experience a transformation in their personality and way of life. They start a new way of life, with a "new heart", new desires and a new outlook. For all intents and proposes they are "born again." They may have been religious before or maybe agnostic or even atheists. In the new life they start after their NDE, they become spiritual. The do not run out to join the nearest church or synagogue. They do not register with a denomination. Rather, in their lives they become more compassionate and loving. They lose the fear of death because they know that death is the beginning of something grand and beautiful.

The Beginning

Dr. Moody in explaining what hundreds of patients shared with him said they have no more fear of death. They have a renewed commitment to loving others, a certain feeling that it is the present that is important, and not worrying about the future. They have a great sense of contentment. Another interesting thing is they show a renewed interest in learning. A few patients, even at an advanced age, when they have recovered, go back to school. They saw in their Life Review the need for learning and improving themselves.

> The full Sequence

The other aspects of the near death experience are not insignificant, but just lower on the scale of significance. Dr. Moody describes the entire process as follows:

The patient's heart stops beating and breathing ceases. The patient has died.

The patient on being revived later, describes floating out of their bodies and seeing exactly what is happening below. In most instances there is emergency methods being applied to save the patient. These activities are described in detail by the patient after. The next steps are often described as indescribable and beyond words to express the feelings and experiences. They enter a tunnel or passageway with a light at the end. They travel through the tunnel to the light. In the light it is beautiful beyond words with feelings of peace and comfort. They meet relatives or friends who died before. Communication does not take place through words, but rather in the form of awareness. They then experience the Life Review during which the question is asked, "What have you done with your life? How have you learned to love?"

Not all patients experience all the events as described. Some never get to the Life Review, while others describe the Life Review as well as conversations with spiritual beings. But all are told at some point they must return and complete their lives on earth. "Your time is not yet. You must return." They then find themselves back in their body with consciousness intact. There are variations of this sequence, but in all instances they experience a separation of consciousness from the natural body.

➤ Two thousand years ago

Two thousand years ago, the experiences we read about today were taking place in the lives of others of that day. Paul, the great evangelist and teacher of Christianity to the Romans and Greeks proclaimed the very same story. In his letter to the church at Corinth he told of a heavenly experience he had. Like many today, he felt uncomfortable speaking about it. He actually confessed that he would rather not talk about it in case others thought more of him than they should. Eventually he conceded and described the experience in his letter to the Corinthian Christians.(*2 Cor. 12*)

➤ Paul's Experience

Paul said his spiritual body or consciousness left his natural body and entered into another dimension. The dimension in which he found himself, could not be described in words. It was beyond human understanding. He found himself in a spiritual world, a "third heaven", where natural law did not apply. He received "an abundance of revelations." This experience was so profound that he did not speak of it for many years. He feared that it might jeopardize the work he had committed his life to. It formed the basis and foundation for his zeal and commitment.

Nevertheless, he often referred to some of the events surrounding his experience. In his letters he constantly referred to a time when a great light shone around him. This occurred during a journey to Damascus to find followers of Jesus and have them imprisoned.

The Damascus road experience brought a dramatic change into Paul's life. Prior to this experience he had been a religious fanatic with much authority in the Jewish religion. He used this authority to seek out the early Christians and imprison them. His intent was to destroy this group who believed that Jesus had been crucified and resurrected. Paul was not your kindest and most compassionate person. The record shows that he stood by uncaring while Stephen, a Christian, was stoned to death.

Just as those who experience an NDE today are transformed after the event, so Paul was transformed and became a messenger for a new kind of life. The kind of life that Jesus had been talking about. He began to spend his life travelling and preaching about the need for a "new heart", with new desires and new attitudes. He emphasized the need for a Higher Consciousness with unconditional love, compassion, joy and peace.

➢ The Central Figure

In the year AD 1 a baby was born in a place called Bethlehem. His life and teachings were destined to change the world. An unknown author summarized his short life of 33 years in this way:

LIFE ONE-0-ONE Find your Purpose

➤ One Solitary Life

He was born in an obscure village.
He worked in a carpenter shop until he was 30.
He then became an itinerant preacher.
He never held an office.
He never had a family or owned a house.
He didn't go to college.
He had no credentials but himself.
He was only 33 when the public turned against Him.
His friends ran away.
He was turned over to his enemies
And went through the mockery of a trial.
He was nailed to a cross between two thieves.
While he was dying, his executioners gambled
For his clothing, the only property He had on earth.
He was laid in a borrowed grave.
Nineteen centuries have come and gone,
And today He is the central figure of the human race.
All the armies that ever marched,
All the navies that ever sailed,
All the parliaments that ever sat,
All the kings the ever reigned,
Have not affected the life of man on this earth as much as that ONE SOLITARY LIFE.

His name was Jesus, and his message was a simple one. Love your neighbour, love your enemy, and love yourself. Fill your life with love. Learn to forgive. Forgive even those who trespass against you.

The Beginning

This was more than those who heard Him could take in. They laughed and scoffed at His teaching. They called Him a dreamer. Finally they killed Him and thought they had closed the chapter on His life. But the most important chapter was yet to take place.

The event that would echo down through the ages, change lives and win hearts was yet to take place. On the third day after his death, he gave his followers evidence that He was still alive. They knew, as he had often told them, only his natural body had died. His spiritual body was still alive. They knew that he had gone to another dimension. A dimension, which you and I will experience when we die. Life is a preparation for that New Day in our lives. We are immortal!